Docker

Complete Guide To Docker

For Beginners And

Intermediates

Craig Berg

Introduction

In the earlier days of technological evolution, developers deployed applications directly on physical machines, with each equipped with an Operating System. Because of the single user-space, applications shared runtime.

Although deployment on physical machines was stable, the maintenance was long and arduous, more so when each host used a different operating system. There was no flexibility for developers and the hosted applications.

As you can imagine, this caused many issues when there was more than one application built that required regular maintenance and a standalone machine for it.

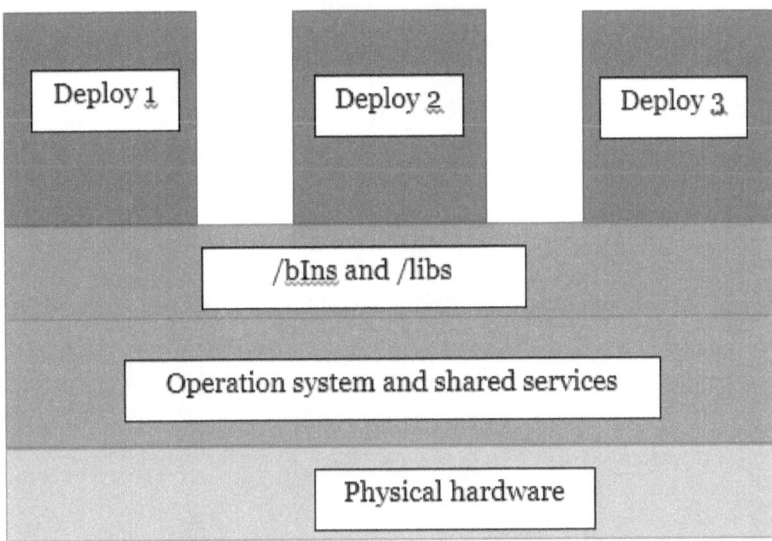

Because of the limitations of deploying applications on physical hardware and utilizing the resources of the entire host system, Virtualization technology came into being, which is when the dynamics of app development started changing.

Using tools known as hypervisors such as Hyper-V, ESX, KVM, VMware, and others, developers started being able to create virtual machines that they could use to deploy host operating systems (guest OS) on one physical machine.

Virtual machines have independent virtual machines, and applications deployed on virtual machines are what we call "isolated and standalone." That means, thanks to the complete isolation of the entire infrastructure running the application, it's possible to perform updates and patches on one instance of the application without affecting other applications.

The diagram below illustrates virtualization.

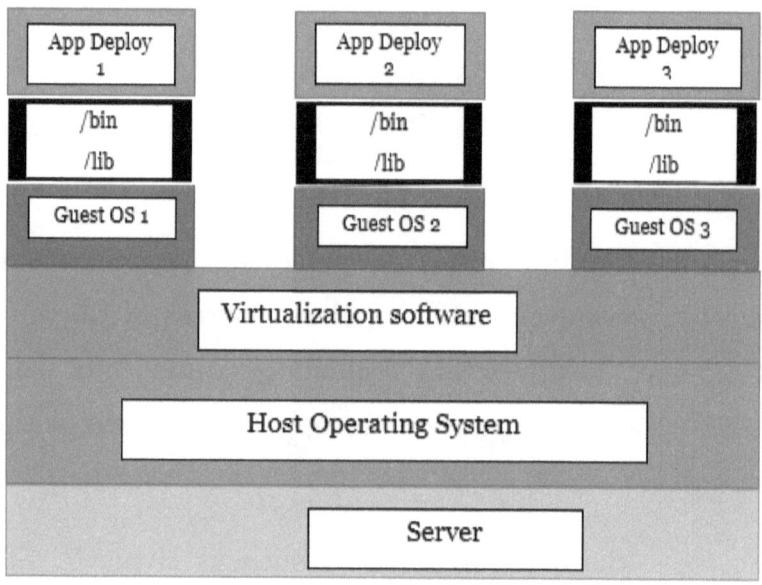

As technology grows, virtual machines, development tools that were once instrumental, are becoming redundant, in part because of the complexity of using Virtual Machines, but mainly because of the technological changes precipitated by the process of reducing hardware emulation. *Containers* are taking over the territory once owned by Virtual Machines.

By using Containers, developers can package applications with their standalone environments. Although compared to VM, Containers are less flexible because they rely on the host operating system; as we will discuss in upcoming chapters, they are a better alternative.

In this Docker guide:

- You will get a concise introduction to the Docker platform and architecture, including how to install it on the Mac, Linux, and Windows OS.

- Learn how to work with Docker Containers, including how to search, list, and pull Docker images.

- We shall look at how to work with Container Network and data management.

And so much, much more.

This guide purposes to equip you with invaluable knowledge that will help you go from "new to Docker," to having the ability to work well with Containers and well on your way to Docker mastery.

Let's get started:

PS: I'd like your feedback. If you are happy with this book, please leave a review on Amazon.

Please leave a review for this book on Amazon by visiting the page below:

https://amzn.to/2VMR5qr

Docker

Your Gift

Let me help you master this and other programming stuff quickly.

Visit

https://bit.ly/codetutorials

To Find Out More

Table of Content

Section 1: Docker Platform And Architecture

Docker is a containerization software developed by Solomon Hykes, the founder of Dot Cloud. It was initially meant to be an internal project. In March 2013, Docker became an open-source software using the Apache License.

Docker utilizes a host's operating system kernel feature that allows containerization. We can illustrate Docker's platform and kernel features using the image below.

Platform	Docker client	Docker compose	Docker sworm	Docker registry
Platform drives	Docker REST interface			
Docker Engine				
Windows OS	Libcontainerd	Libnetwork	Graph	Plugins
Linux OS	Containered + rumC			
Windows OS	Computer services			
	Control groups (job objects)	Namespaces (Networking, process table, obi Namespaces	Layer functionalities (Registry, nion like Fs extensions)	Other Functionalities
Linus OS	Control Groups (vgroups)	Namespaces (pid, mnt, net, ipc)	Layer functionalities (Device manager, zfs, vfs, union fileststem	Other functionalities

To help you develop a deeper understanding of Docker better, let's look at the facets that make up its core architecture:

Namespaces

Namespaces are the main building blocks of Docker Containers. There are various types of namespaces, with one of them acting as an isolating block from one application to another. The creation of Namespaces happens through the clone system call. Developers sometimes also attach existing namespaces. Some of the namespaces used by Docker include:

- The PID namespace

- The net namespace

- IPC namespace

- UTS namespace

- MNT namespace

- User namespace

Let's discuss each of the above namespaces in detail:

The PID Namespace

The PID namespaces in Linux system isolates the process Identification Number space. That means processes using different PID namespaces can have the same PID.

The PID namespace allows containers to deliver functionalities like suspending and resuming the set of processes within the container. It also gives developers the ability to migrate the container from one host to another while the processes running within the container maintain their original PIDs.

PIDs in a new PID namespace start at 1, somewhat like a standalone system, and calls to `fork`, `vfork`, or `clone` will produce processes with PIDs that are unique within the namespace.

As mentioned, the PID namespaces allow each container to have an isolated set of PIDs. Each PID creates a unique process hierarchy.

A "parent" (main) namespace can manage the "children" namespaces and perform actions to alter their functionality. A child namespace, however, cannot see or perform any particular action on the parent namespace node.

Other than the initial ("root") PID namespace, each of the nested namespaces has a parent. The parent in this case refers to the PID namespace of the process that actually created the namespace using `unshare` or `clone`. Thus, the PID namespaces make some sort of tree that contains all all namespaces that ultimately trace their ancestry to the root namespace.

If there are two levels of hierarchy, then at the top level, we would see the process running inside the child namespace with a different PID. Therefore, a process running within a child namespace usually has two PIDs: one for the parent namespace and one for the child namespace.

Let me give an illustration: If we start a program such as `nano`, the action creates a parent and child process:

```
nano init.conf

sudo ps aux | grep nano

bash          525   0.3   0.0   15672   3260 tty1
T     23:18    0:00 nano init.conf

bash          527   0.0   0.0   14120   1156 tty1
S     23:18    0:00 grep nano
```

You can find more information on PID namespace from the resource page below:

http://man7.org/linux/man-
pages/man7/pid_namespaces.7.html

The NET Namespace

The network namespace is a logical copy of the network stack. It has individual building blocks like firewall rules, network interfaces, and routing tables.

The default location for the network namespaces is:

`/var/run/netns/NAME`

By convention, a process usually inherits all its network namespace from the parent namespace, where, initially, the same namespace from the `init` process is shared by all processes.

By using the PID namespace only, we can run one program more than once in isolated environments. For example, we can run a service such as NGINX on different containers since the PIDs do not conflict, but we cannot communicate with the service on port 80 without using the net namespace.

The net namespaces make it possible to create multiple network interfaces on every container, thus allowing services to communicate on their respective ports. It is also good to note that loopback addresses on each container are unique.

For networking to occur within the containers, a special pair of network interfaces are created in two different net namespaces, allowing communication with each interface. Each interface resides inside a container, and the other resides inside a host operating system. The interface in the container is eth0, and the host interface gets allocated a random but unique name.

The interfaces interlink via a network bridge, which, in most cases, is docker0 that allows the communication between the container and the packets routes.

To learn more about the net namespace, check the Linux programmers page available here.

http://man7.org/linux/man-pages/man8/ip-netns.8.html

The IPC Namespace

The IPC or inter-communication namespace helps isolate and provide System V IPC objects like semaphores, shared memory segments, and POSIX message ques within a system. Although the use of the IPC namespace is not common today, older, and even some new processes, still depend on it.

An IPC resource initialized by one container can be consumed or terminated by another container. If this happens, the application tied to the IPC resource on the first container fails. That is where the IPC namespace comes in hand: it prevents processes running in one namespace from accessing other resources of another IPC namespace.

The USER Namespace.

The USER namespace isolates the security-based identifiers and attributes within a unique user ID or group ID. It is possible to nest user namespaces. Except for the "root" or initial namespace, each user namespace has a primary or parent user namespace and as many child user namespaces it needs (sometimes none).

The parent user namespace is the user namespace of the process that creates the user namespace via a call to `unshare` or `clone` with the `CLONE_NEWUSER` flag.

Since the user namespace allows for the mapping of users and groups per namespace instance, therefore, using the user namespace, it makes it possible to have users with a zero identifier within a container and users with non-zero identifiers on the host.

The UTS Namespace

The Linux UTS namespace provides an idea isolation mechanism for two system hostname and NIS domain name identifiers.

Linux users can retrieve the identifiers using the `uname`, `gethostname` or `getdomainname`. To set the identifiers, you can use the `sethostname` or `setdomainname`.

Any changes done on either variable become globally broadcasted and reflected on all processes in the same UTS namespace but not to other processes in other namespaces.

Thus, the UTS namespace allows developers to assign different hostnames on a single container. For more information on Linux UTS namespaces, check the following resource page:

http://man7.org/linux/man-pages/man7/uts_namespaces.7.html

The MNT Namespace

Linux Systems use the MNT or mount namespaces to provide isolation for the list of mount points available to the processes in a single namespace instance. We create a mount namespace by using `clone` or `unshare` with the `CLONE_NEWNS` flag.

Without the `mnt` namespace, you can only use the `chroot` operation to check the relative paths of a particular system from a chrooted `directory/namespace`.

However, with the `mnt` namespace, a single container can have its own individual set of mounted root directories and filesystem tree.

It's worth noting that processes from one `mnt` namespace cannot interact with a mounted filesystem of another `mnt` namespace.

Cgroups

Control groups, also called `cgroups`, refers to a feature that allows processes within a Linux System to be arrangeable in hierarchical groups. These groups make it possible to monitor and limit the usage of various resources on the system.

The `cgroup` interface in the kernel is available courtesy of a pseudo-filesystem called `cgroupfs`. The execution of the grouping mechanism occurs in the core kernel group code, and the resource monitoring and limiting is possible because of a set of per-resource-type subsystems such as Memory, CPU, etc.

`Cgroups` provide resource monitoring and limitation features for containers. They're comparable to the `ulimit` and `setrlimit` system calls.

However, instead of performing limitations to a single process within the system, the `cgroups` makes it possible to perform limitations on a group of operations to various resources on a single system.

Control groups divide further into various subsystems such as Memory, CPU, CPU sets Input/Output memory blocks, Freezers, etc. Linux subsystems are usable independently but are also groupable.

A subsystem refers to a kernel component that modifies the original behavior in a `cgroup`; we can also call them controllers or resource controllers.

Control groups for a resource controller (a subsystem) are set in a hierarchical paradigm defined by either CRUD (create, rename, or removing) directories with the `cgroup` filesystem.

Control groups provide features such as:

- **Accounting**: This feature allows users to monitor and measure resource usage for various subsystems; the use of this feature is routine in billing.

- **Resource Limitation:** This feature allows users to bound control groups to a specific subsystem, thus allowing the processes in the specified `cgroup` to run on the set subsystem.

- **Control**: The Cgroups feature makes it possible to perform actions such as freezing and performing restarts on groups.

- **Priority:** Control groups also have features that allow for prioritization, allowing you to allocate higher or lower subsystem share to some groups.

The main subsystems that are directly manageable by the control groups include:

- **CPU:** The CPU limits are directly manageable by the groups.

- **Memory:** Control groups can set limits on memory usage by the processes in the `cgroups`.

- **Freezer:** The groups can also suspend or resume processes in a group

- **Blkio:** The block IO controller sets Input/Output access to and from the block devices within the system such as storage devices, etc.

- **Cpuacct:** The CPU accounting controller groups tasks by using the cgroups and account for the CPU usage of the tasks. That means the `cpuacct` subsystem generates the CPU utilization report.

- **Cpusets:** Cpusets provide a mechanism for assigning a set of CPUs and Memory Nodes to a set of tasks. Cgroups uses the `cpusets` subsystem to assign CPUs on multicore systems to various tasks in a group.

- **Devices**: Control groups also manage the devices, granting or denying access to tasks within a group.

There are various ways to control work when working with `cgroups`. The most common way is to access the cgroups via the virtual `cgroup` filesystem (`cgroupfs`) or by accessing it using the `libcgroup` library packages.

View the cgroups in the `/sys/fs/cgroup directory`.

You can install the `libcgroup` package on Debian using the following command:

```
sudo apt-get update && sudo apt-get install cgroup-tools -y
```

Once you have the packages installed, you can view the mounted subsystems and their mount points in the pseudo filesystem using the following command:

```
$ lssubsys -M
cpuset /sys/fs/cgroup/cpuset
cpu,cpuacct /sys/fs/cgroup/cpu,cpuacct
blkio /sys/fs/cgroup/blkio
memory /sys/fs/cgroup/memory

memory /sys/fs/cgroup/memory
devices /sys/fs/cgroup/devices
freezer /sys/fs/cgroup/freezer
net_cls,net_prio
/sys/fs/cgroup/net_cls,net_prio
perf_event /sys/fs/cgroup/perf_event
pids /sys/fs/cgroup/pids
rdma /sys/fs/cgroup/rdma
```

Let's discuss the union filesystem.

The Union Filesystem

To gain a better understanding of the composition of Docker containers, we will have to understand the Union filesystem first, which, although steeped in technicalities, is fundamental to understand.

Most GNU Linux and Unix users are aware that, except for individual regular files, almost everything in the system appears as a file. System devices in the file system also appear as files under `/dev/device_name`.

A formatted partition —meaning it has a filesystem such as NFTS, FAT, FAT32, EXT fat, etc.— has to mounted on the system so that you can interact with it. The process of mounting involves attaching the file system on a logical file to a specific directory within the system tree, which is where the Union File system comes into play. The UNION file system concept comes from sets and sets theory in mathematics.

You can read more about sets and sets theory from the following resource:

https://en.wikipedia.org/wiki/Union_(set_theory)

Let take an example where you mount two file systems on a single mount point of a system.

Without using the UNION file system, you will only see the files of the mount point you mounted last. The UNION file system allows us to view all the contents of mounted file systems on a single mount point.

Docker

The UNION filesystem works by mounting the files and directories of various file systems (also known as layers) and creating a new virtual file system.

Docker uses the UNION mounting system by overlaying all the layers attached to a specific image and initializing a read-only filesystem while starting a container. Docker also creates a new read-only layer that the container runtime environment uses.

Docker uses various flavors of the Union filesystem. These include DeviceMapper, overlay1, overlay2, ZFS, AUFS, etc. Docker also creates a virtual file system storage driver that does not support copy-on-write.

It's worth noting that the VFS is not a UNION filesystem. The VFS driver means that the layer within the file system is a directory, and the new layer created requires a deep copy of the existing parent layer. That often leads to low performance and increased disk usage—however, its stable and works in most environments.

Container Format

The Docker Engine encapsulates the UnionFS, control groups and namespaces into a single wrapper referred to as a container format.

`libcontainer` is the default container format.

Now that you know more about the Docker platform and its base architecture, let's move on and learn how to install Docker on various systems:

Section 2: Installing Docker On Windows, Linux (Debian-Based), And Osx

In this section, we are going to cover how to set up Docker on various platforms.

We are going to use Debian Buster for Linux illustrations, Windows 10 for Windows Illustration, and the Google Cloud Platform for cloud-based Docker instances. Docker has support on most Linux distributions, including REHL flavors, ARCH, Gentoo, Ubuntu, Fedora, and many others.

Let us first see the requirements for setting up Docker on our local machines.

System Requirements

For Windows users, the following are the recommended requirements:

- Windows 10 build 1506 or higher

- A 64-bit, Intel or AMD processor

- At least 4 GB of memory. For smoother performance, it's better to have 8 GB of memory or and higher.

- Hardware-level virtualization enabled. You can use the system BIOS to enable VT-X on your local machine.

If you are using Linux, you can check the system requirements for your favorite distribution below.

NOTE: Debian users must have at least 4 GB of RAM and running Debian 10 Buster or Debian 9 Stretch. Your system should also be running on a 64-bit architecture since Docker does not support x-86 architecture.

CentOS:

https://docs.docker.com/engine/install/centos/

Ubuntu and Ubuntu-based distributions:

https://docs.docker.com/engine/install/ubuntu/

Debian and Raspbian Distributions:

https://docs.docker.com/engine/install/debian/

Fedora:

https://docs.docker.com/engine/install/fedora/

To check the architecture of your current system. Use the command:

```
uname -i
$ uname -i
x86_64
```

The system should also be running kernel version 3.8 or higher. Check the kernel version using the command:

```
uname -r
4.4.0-97-generic
```

You can also check for supported storage backends such as DeviceMapper, VFS, AUFS, ZFS, and Overlay filesystem. Systems such as Ubuntu may use Overlay FS.

Most Linux distributions should have device-mapper thin-provisioning module for implementing the layers. To check whether you have device-mapper installed on your distro, use the command.

```
dmsetup -ls
```

Finally, you should ensure you've enabled support for namespaces and cgroups. Since most Linux distributions have made them available and supported for a while, your Linux distro should have that support in-built. To check cgroups and namespaces, check the kernel configuration file using the command:

```
cat              /boot/config-4.4.0-97-generic
CONFIG_NAMESPACES=y | grep -i namespaces

cat              /boot/config-4.4.0-97-generic
CONFIG_CGROUPS=y | grep -i cgroups
```

For smooth experiences, Mac users should have the following system requirements.

- The Mac hardware must be a 2010 or newer model

- macOS must be version 10.13 or later.

- At least 4 GB of RAM.

- You should have VirtualBox versions 4.3.30 or later installed on your system; earlier versions are not compatible with Docker Desktop

How To Install Docker Desktop On Windows

We are going to install Docker on our local Windows OS-based machine using the Docker desktop installer. The installer has the Docker engine, the Docker client, Docker Compose, Kubernetes, and Credential Helper.

NOTE: Docker containers created using the Docker desktop are sharable with all the user accounts available on the installation host. That's because Windows user accounts use the same VM to run the containers.

First, open your browser and navigate to:

https://www.docker.com/products/docker-desktop

Once on the landing page, download the docker desktop installer for windows.

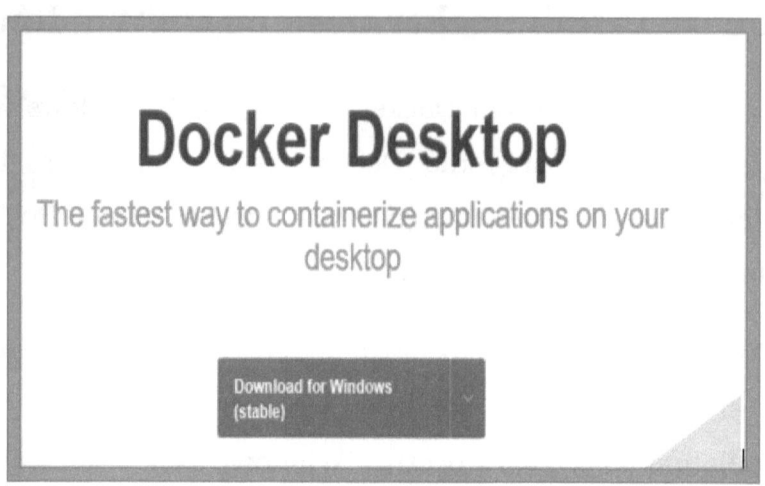

As a recommendation, enable Hyper-V features before the installation. If not enabled, you can allow the Docker installer to enable it for you.

Once downloaded, start the installer and allow it to download any required packages.

During the installation, select "Enable Hyper-V Windows features." Selecting this feature will require a reboot after installation.

Once the installation completes, click close, if required, reboot your computer, and start Docker.

How To Run Docker Desktop

Once the installation completes and you have everything set up, click on the Docker desktop icon on the desktop or open from the start menu to launch Docker.

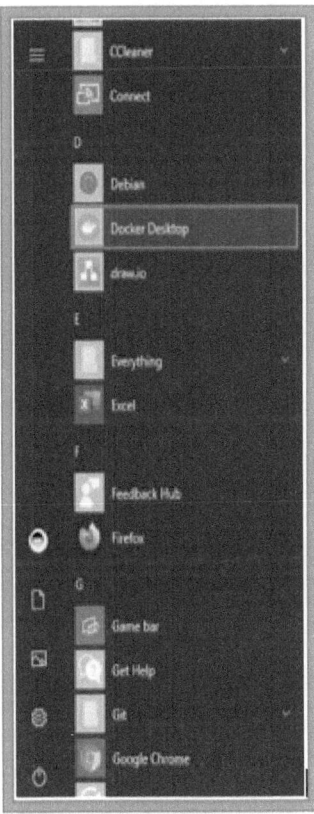

NOTE: For initialization, ensure you have at least 2 GB of free memory to avoid any errors.

Once successfully initialized, you will get a Docker welcome screen that has a tutorial on how to build your first Docker image. We will cover this in later sections of the book, but feel free to experiment.

How To Install Docker On Mac OS

The Docker desktop installer for Mac also comes coupled with the Docker engine, Docker client, and all the packages included in the Windows installer.

Open your browser and navigate to the following URL:

https://hub.docker.com/editions/community/docker-ce-desktop-mac

Once on the landing page, download the docker installer for mac.

Once downloaded, open the docker.dmg file to open the installer and drag the docker icon to the Applications folder on your system.

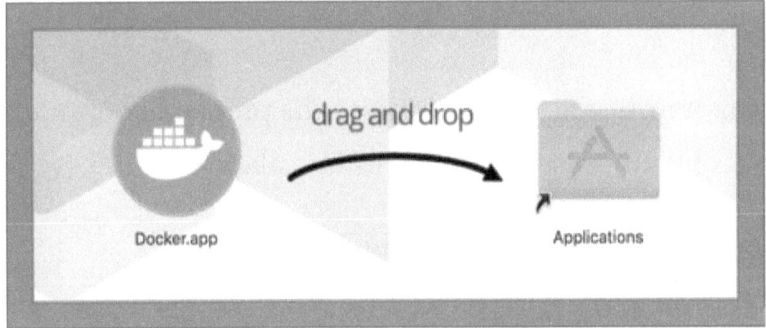

To start Docker, click on the docker icon in the Applications folder and wait for initialization. Once Docker is running, you will get a welcome window with a starter tutorial.

Installing Docker On Linux (Debian Buster)

Before installing Docker on Linux, ensure you are using a system that meets the requirements listed earlier.

Next, we need to remove all previous installations of Docker on the system. The names of docker installations might include: `docker.io` `docker-engine,` `Docker,` `containerd, runc`

Open the terminal and enter the command below:

```
sudo apt-get remove docker.io Docker, docker-engine -y
```

We can now install Docker without the probability of running into problems caused by previous installations.

In the terminal, start by executing the command:

```
sudo   apt-get   install   curl   ca-certificates
apt-transport-https      software-properties-
common gnupg-agent -y
```

Next, we add the docker GPG key using the command:

```
curl                                          -fsSL
https://download.docker.com/linux/debain/gpg
 | sudo apt-key add -
```

Next, verify that you are using the Docker official key with fingerprint:

```
9DC8 5822 9FC7 DD38 854A   E2D8 8D81 803C 0EBF
CD88
```

Use the command below to search the last characters of the key and verify:

```
sudo apt-key fingerprint 0EBFCD88

pub    rsa4096 2017-02-22 [SCEA]

       9DC8 5822 9FC7 DD38 854A   E2D8 8D81
803C 0EBF CD88

uid              [ unknown] Docker Release (CE
deb) <docker@docker.com>

sub    rsa4096 2017-02-22 [S]
```

The next step is to add the docker apt repository to the stable repository channel. Use the commands below:

```
$ sudo add-apt-repository \

   "deb                       [arch=amd64]
https://download.docker.com/linux/debian \

   $(lsb_release -cs) \

   stable"
```

If you prefer frequent updates, you can use the `nightly` test channel by changing the `stable` value to `test` in the above command.

NOTE: Nightly channel may have a few bugs.

Now we can install Docker engine using the command below:

```
sudo apt-get update && sudo apt-get install
docker-ce docker-ce-cli containerd.io -y
```

Once the installation completes, verify that the installation is working using the command:

```
docker container run hello-world
```

You can also configure the docker daemon to start during boot time using the `systemctl`

Start the docker service using the command `sudo systemctl start docker`

Enable the docker service at startup using the command: `sudo systemctl enable Docker`

Stop the service with `sudo systemctl stop Docker`.

How To Use A Script To Automate Docker Install

In most cases, you will need to setup docker on a single host, which is a relatively simple process. However, if you need to setup Docker on hundreds of hosts, the task will be repetitive and tedious. You can use a script to automate this process.

Open the command prompt and start a new bash file. Ensure you are comfortable with what the script does before executing it. You will require sudo or root permissions.

Navigate to the following URL:

https://get.docker.com

Once there, copy the script and save it. Once done as saved, execute the file using the command:

```
sudo chmod +x docker.sh && sudo ./docker.sh
```

Section 3: How to Pull Docker Images and Run Containers

This section intends to test whether Docker is running as expected, not to explain the concepts. We will cover the entire Docker workflow in later sections.

We will start by pulling a docker image and running a container using the image. If you prefer to using the graphical interface provided by Docker desktop, we will be using the commands throughout the book. To avoid potential errors, ensure that Docker daemon is running. Open the terminal and enter the command:

```
$ docker image pull nginx

Using the default tag: latest

latest: Pulling from library/nginx

afb6ec6fdc1c:          Pull          complete
b90c53a0b692:          Pull          complete
11fa52a0fdc0:          Pull          complete
Digest:
sha256:30dfa439718a17baafefadf16c5e7c9d0a1cde
97b4fd84f63b69e13513be7097

Status:    Downloaded    newer    image    for
nginx:latest

docker.io/library/nginx:latest
```

Once you have the image downloaded, you can view the list of images using the command:

```
docker image ls
REPOSITORY                                  TAG
IMAGE ID          CREATED                   SIZE

nginx                                       latest
9beeba249f3e      10 days ago              127MB

docker/getting-started                      latest
3c156928aeec               5  weeks  ago
24.8MB
```

```
To   create   a   docker   container   using   a
downloaded image, use the command:
```

```
docker     container     run     -id     -name
<preferred_name> <image_name>
```

For example, to create an Nginx container, we use the command:

```
docker     container     run     -id     -name     nginx-
container nginx
```

To view the containers created, use the command:

```
$ docker container ls

CONTAINER    ID                              IMAGE
COMMAND                              CREATED
STATUS              PORTS              NAMES

6fa253a43c4b                              nginx
"nginx  -g  'daemon  of…"      29  seconds  ago
Up    26    seconds                      80/tcp
nginx-container

$ docker container ls
```

Docker uses a client-server architecture. The Docker binary has the Docker client and the Docker server daemon that exist in a single host.

The Docker client can communicate with a local or remote docker server daemon via the network sockets or RESTful API clients. The docker server daemon is responsible for performing tasks such as building, running, and distributing containers.

The docker client daemon sends commands to the docker server daemon that is running on a remote or localhost, which then connects to the Docker registry to get the images requested by the docker client.

In our simple example above, the docker client installed with the docker binary communicates with the docker server daemon that then connects to the docker registry requesting an NGINX image. Once downloaded or found, we can use it to create containers.

A docker image refers to a read-only template used to create containers during runtime. Docker image templates depend on the base image and all the layers residing in it.

A docker registry stores the docker images; the by docker daemon references it when pulling images. Docker registries can be public or private; it all depends on the specified setting and the location of pulling and pushing the images. Public docker images are available in the Docker hub.

An image repository refers to a collection of a similar set of images distinguished by their GUIDs. For example, you can install various versions of nginx image by passing the tag such as `docker image pull nginx:latest` where `latest` becomes substituted with the correct version.

Containers refer to "virtual machines" that run base containers and the accompanying layers. Containers have all the requirements for running applications on them.

A Docker registry index manages accounts, searches, tags, permissions, etc. in a public docker image registry.

Docker

The concept is illustratable using the following image:

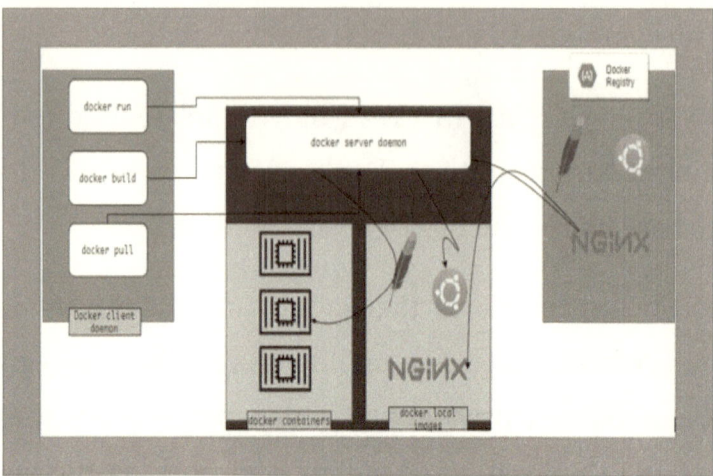

Let's move on to the next section and learn how to work with containers:

Section 4: Working With Docker Containers

In this section, we are going to cover Docker containers in more detail. We will cover how to search and pull images, list and manage containers, manage container logs, remove containers, stop containers, and so much more.

In the previous section, we illustrated a simple process of creating containers using Docker. As the primary goal of Docker is to create containers, this section shall delve a bit deeper into that.

Getting comfortable with performing tasks such as creating, updating, stopping, and deleting containers will allow you to utilize the full functionalities of Docker.

Before getting started, let us make sure that Docker is up and running by using the command-line utility to get the docker version. If not running, you will get an error close to the one shown below:

Docker

```
Client: Docker Engine - Community
 Version:           19.03.8
 API version:       1.40
 Go version:        go1.12.17
 Git commit:        afacb8b
 Built:             Wed Mar 11 01:23:10 2020
 OS/Arch:           windows/amd64

Experimental:      false
error       during       connect:      Get
http://%2F%2F.%2Fpipe%2Fdocker_engine/v1.40/v
ersion:   open  //./pipe/docker_engine:  The
system cannot find the file specified. In the
default daemon configuration on Windows, the
docker  client  must  be  run  elevated  to
connect. This  error  may  also  indicate  that
the docker daemon is not running.
```

Once Docker is running, you will get an output displaying the
client and server versions as well as other detailed
information.

Docker

```
Client: Docker Engine - Community
Version:           19.03.8
 API version:       1.40
 Go version:        go1.12.17
 Git commit:        afacb8b
 Built:             Wed Mar 11 01:23:10 2020
 OS/Arch:           windows/amd64
 Experimental:      false


Server: Docker Engine - Community
 Engine:
  Version:          19.03.8


  API version:       1.40  (minimum  version
1.12)
  Go version:       go1.12.17
  Git commit:       afacb8b
  Built:            Wed Mar 11 01:29:16 2020
  OS/Arch:          linux/amd64
  Experimental:     false
 containerd:
  Version:          v1.2.13
  GitCommit:
7ad184331fa3e55e52b890ea95e65ba581ae3429
 runc:
  Version:          1.0.0-rc10
  GitCommit:
dc9208a3303feef5b3839f4323d9beb36df0a9dd
 docker-init:
  Version:          0.18.0
  GitCommit:        fec3683
```

```
 API version:          1.40 (minimum version
1.12)

 Go version:           go1.12.17

 Git commit:           afacb8b
```

How To Search And List Images In Docker

To start creating a docker container, we need an image to use. If you know the name of the image, you can pull the image using the docker pull command.

We can also search the docker registry that holds both private and public images for the target we are looking for:

By convention, docker search is executed on the docker public registry that is available at:

https://hub.docker.com

To search an image in the Docker registry, we use the **docker search** command that uses the following syntax.

```
docker search [option flags] [term]
```

Docker search options that are available in the official documentation include:

Options:

  -f, --filter filter   Filter output based on conditions provided

     --format string   Pretty-print search using a Go template

     --limit int   Max number of search results (default 25)

     --no-trunc Don't truncate output

For example, if we want to search for a Debian or Nginx image, we use the command:

```
docker search -limit 8 debian
```

```
NAME                          DESCRIPTION
STARS                          OFFICIAL
AUTOMATED

ubuntu                         Ubuntu is a
Debian-based Linux operating sys...    10932
[OK]

debian                         Debian is a
Linux distribution that's compos...    3495
[OK]

arm32v7/debian                 Debian is a
Linux distribution that's compos...    66

itscaro/debian-ssh             debian:jessie
28                                     [OK]

samueldebruyn/debian-git          a minimal
docker container with debian and g...   22
[OK]

eboraas/debian                 Debian base
images, for all currently-availa...      8
[OK]

smartentry/debian             debian with
smartentry                              4
[OK]

jdub/debian-sources-resource   Concourse CI
resource to check for updated D...       0
[OK]
```

51

The docker search output gives information related to the Debian images such as the names, descriptions, number of star ratings given to the images. It also provides information about whether an image is official or not, as well as its automation status.

The name shows the official name allocated to the image. The name uses the user/image-name naming convention.

The stars show how many users have liked the given image and how popular it is. The official status, on the other hand, shows whether the listed image is from a trusted source or not. The Automated status shows whether the image is built automatically once it's pushed into a version control system or not.

You can also pass the –filter option to show only automated images or with a rating of a particular range as well as whether an image is official or not.

```
docker  search  --filter  is-automated=true  --
filter stars=10 debian

itscaro/debian-ssh                debian:jessie
28                                        [OK]

samueldebruyn/debian-git    a minimal docker
container with debian and g…   22 [OK]
```

How To Pull Docker Images

To download images from the docker registry or repository, we use the docker pull command. The general syntax for docker pull is;

```
docker pull [OPTIONS] NAME[:TAG|@DIGEST]
```

The previous section of the book illustrated an example of downloading an Nginx image from the repository.

The docker pull command works by downloading all the layers of the image from the repository or registry and create the image locally.

As mentioned earlier, image tags help classify groups of images of the same type. For example, a Debian image flavor such as Debian 10 can is installable using the correct tag name.

The command below shows how to install Debian buster using the tags available in the docker registry.

```
docker pull debian: unstable-20200514
```

This downloads the Debian image tagged with the passed tag name. To view that tags available for your specific image, open:

https://hub.docker.com/ /image name?tab=tags

Newer version of Docker give developers the ability to pull images using a content-addressable identifier commonly called a digest. It helps dockers to work with specific images rather than tags.

Once a docker image becomes downloaded to the localhost, it goes into storage in the local storage cache, allowing future pulls of the same image to be quick.

How To Get The Downloaded Images

To view the list of all the images in the local system, we use the `docker images ls command`. The images existing in the system may have either been created by the Dockerfile or pulled from the docker registry using the **Docker pull** command.

Ensure that the docker daemon is running before executing the commands. To view all the images available in our system, use the command:

```
docker images or docker images ls

$ sudo docker images
```

REPOSITORY	TAG	IMAGE
ID	CREATED	SIZE
tomcat	latest	
1b6b1fe7261e	9 days ago	647MB
mariadb	latest	
9c1f27148b1f	10 days ago	357MB
nginx	latest	
9beeba249f3e	10 days ago	127MB
httpd	latest	
d4e60c8eb27a	10 days ago	166MB
debian	latest	
5971ee6076a0	11 days ago	114MB
centos	centos7	
b5b4d78bc90c	2 weeks ago	203MB
cassandra	latest	
604151722441	4 weeks ago	379MB
hello-world	latest	
bf756fb1ae65	4 months ago	
13.3kB		

Using the docker client, we request the docker daemon to retrieve all the images pulled to the host. It's also good to note that the images with similar names are downloaded and stored with the same names but different tags.

How To Initialize Containers

Having pulled the images from the repository, we can use the images to create containers. To create a docker container, we use the command docker container run. The general syntax for the command is:

```
docker container run [OPTIONS] IMAGE [COMMAND]
[ARG...]
```

Let us create a docker container using an image of our choice. How about a CentOS 7 container?

```
$ sudo docker run -t -i --name cento7-
container centos /bin/bash

[root@7b0bc4c20fcc /]#
```

In the docker run command, we passed the -i (interactive) option that initializes the specified container in interactive mode and keeps the Standard Input open.

The -t flag or the -tty option allocates the pseudo-tty and attaches to the STDIN

Now we can interact with the CentOS container we created, use the command exit, or press CTRL + D to exit to the main host. You can also detach from the container using the command `docker container detach` that exits to the main docker shell. To interact with the container again, use the `docker container attach` command.

The actions performed by Docker under the hood include:

- Merging all the layers from the image used using Union Filesystem

- Allocation unique identifiers to the containers

- Allocating a filesystem and mounting the read/writer layers for the containers

- Provision of a bridge network interfaces.

- Internet Protocol address assigned to the container

- Performing commands specified by the users.

In our case, the commands specified by the user are /bin/bash that allows us to interact with the system directly.

Container specific information such as the hostname, logs and configuration details are in storage under **/var/lib/docker/containers**

By default, the docker run command automatically initializes and starts the docker container. However, you can create and start the docker container later using the commands

```
$ id = $(docker container create -t -i debian /bin/bash )
$ docker container start -i -a $id
```

Using these commands starts the container in the background, which then becomes attachable. You can also start a container in the background by passing the -d flag in the docker run command.

You can also choose to delete a container automatically once it exits using the rm flag as shown in the command below:

```
docker run -t -i -rm debian /bin/bash
```

Once you exit the interactive shell, the container becomes destroyed automatically.

To get more information on how to use the **docker run -options**, use the docker documentation or **docker run -help** command in the terminal.

https://docs.docker.com/engine/reference/commandline/container_run/

How To Get Containers In A Docker

To view all the docker containers, both running and stopped, we use the **docker container ls** command. The general syntax for the command is:

```
docker container ls [OPTIONS]
```

For example, to view all the containers in the host:

```
$ sudo docker container ls -a
CONTAINER     ID                              IMAGE
COMMAND                              CREATED
STATUS                              PORTS
NAMES


7b0bc4c20fcc                              centos
"/bin/bash"                  2   hours   ago
Exited        (127)      2    hours        ago
cento7-container

cf6dfce19daf                         hello-world
"/hello"                     2   hours   ago
Exited        (0)        2    hours        ago
jolly_moore
```

Once we run the docker container ls command, the docker daemon fetches the metadata associated with the containers. Unless specified, the **Docker container ls** command returns the following metadata information about the containers.

- The containers Unique identifier also called container ID.

- The name of the container

- The image used by the container

- The command executed immediately after creating the container

- Detailed time about its creation

- The current status of the container – running or stopped

- The ports exposed in the container

The docker container ls command also accepts arguments that allow you to control the output. For example, to get only the container ids, you can use the command;

```
docker container ls -aq
```

You can also pass the –filter followed by the arguments to filter output from the command.

More information on container ls command is available on the official documentation available on the resource page below:

https://docs.docker.com/engine/reference/commandline/container_ls/

How To Work With Container Logs

Docker containers create logs on STDIN/STDOUT that are accessible without logging in the container. Using the command docker container log, we can view the container logs. The general syntax for the command is

docker container logs [OPTIONS] [CONTAINER_NAME]

For example, to view the logs for a debian container, we use the command:

```
$ sudo docker container logs debian

root@2ab3e6bc0c61:/# exit

exit
```

Once we execute the command, Docker searches for the container's specific logs under:

```
/var/lib/docker          /containers/Container
ID/Container-ID-json.log/
```

To add more functionality to the logs output, use the command flags such as -t that displays the time stamps for the logs. Another useful flag is the -f that shows tail-like behavior.

To find more information about the docker container log command, use the documentations or **docker container logs -help**

How To Stop And Destroy Docker Containers

We can stop one or more running containers at once using the docker container stop command. The general syntax for the command is:

```
docker container stop [OPTIONS] [CONTAINER1]
[CONTAINER2] [CONTAINER...n]
```

To stop the Debian container, we created in earlier sections, use the command:

```
sudo docker container stop debian

debian
```

Once we call the stop command, Docker automatically moves the container from running state to the stopped state that works by stopping all the processes within the containers.

To stop all running containers, execute the following commands

```
Docker stop $(docker ps -q)
```

For example, list all the containers and then stop them:

You can find more information on docker stop command on the official documentation available here:

https://docs.docker.com/engine/reference/commandline/container_stop/

We can completely remove a container using the docker rm command. Before removing a container, you have to stop the container; alternatively, you can use the force option. The standard syntax is:

```
sudo docker container rm [OPTIONS] CONTAINER
[CONTAINER_name]
```

Docker

For example, let us remove all the containers in our host. First, we will start by listing all the containers.

```
sudo docker container ls -a
```

```
CONTAINER   ID                          IMAGE
COMMAND                        CREATED
STATUS                         PORTS
NAMES

393c7eb86e69                          nginx
"nginx  -g  'daemon  of…"    11  minutes  ago
Exited      (0)      8        minutes      ago
nginx-server

7aff06d18fc0                          httpd
"httpd-foreground"           13  minutes  ago
Exited      (0)      13       minutes      ago
apache

9ba38e870390                          mariadb
"docker-entrypoint.s…"       14  minutes  ago
Exited      (1)      14       minutes      ago
mariadb

2ab3e6bc0c61                          debian
"/bin/bash"                  28  minutes  ago
Exited      (0)      28       minutes      ago
debian

7b0bc4c20fcc                          centos
"/bin/bash"                  13  hours  ago
Exited      (127)    12       hours      ago
cento7-container

cf6dfce19daf                          hello-world
"/hello"                     13  hours  ago
Exited      (0)      13       hours      ago
jolly_moore
```

Next, call the docker container rm with –force if the containers are running, followed by the list of containers to remove, as shown below:

```
sudo docker rm --force nginx-server apache
debian mariadb centos-container

nginx-server

apache

debian

mariadb
```

You can also choose to remove the links and the volumes associated with the container. The docker rm command works by removing the read/write layer created at the first initialization of the container.

You can also remove all the stopped containers at once. Let us start by creating containers, stopping them, and removing them all at once.

```
sudo docker run --name debian debian:latest

sudo docker run --name nginx nginx:latest
```

Next, ensure that the status of the container is exited and then remove them using the docker prune command:

```
sudo docker container ls -a
```

CONTAINER   ID   IMAGE
COMMAND   CREATED
STATUS   PORTS
NAMES

859c5614dac1   nginx:latest "nginx -g
'daemon of..." About a minute ago   Exited (0)
15 seconds ago   nginx

a3eda9a171ed   debian:latest
"bash"   2 minutes ago
Exited   (0)   2   minutes   ago
debian

7b0bc4c20fcc   centos
"/bin/bash"   13 hours ago
Exited   (127)   13   hours   ago
cento7-container

cf6dfce19daf   hello-world
"/hello"   13 hours ago
Exited   (0)   13   hours   ago
jolly_moore

And finally, we can remove the containers:

```
sudo docker container prune
```

WARNING! This will remove all stopped
containers.

Are you sure you want to continue? [y/N] Y

Deleted Containers:

859c5614dac1c72b84e0cd0b3b8a6f06e701e867787d6
b54b4583cc140f13e03

a3eda9a171ed0e61ab3e1e21fb778efebe65ab3abd440
a881d8f633af26895b2

7b0bc4c20fcc620418ac216b683aa5a2d8b8c293edd5b
5fe48e3d649899d3cd8

cf6dfce19dafd879b465afa72fe410c6bb9190b8d8760
64883cf61b710f099a4

Total reclaimed space: 33B

Container Failure Actions

In older versions of Docker, at the reboot of a docker host or if a container failed for a particular reason, the containers required manual rebooting using the restart command. On newer versions, Docker allows us to set restart actions upon failure or host reboot.

The restart policy for a specific container is specified using the docker run command. The general syntax is:

```
docker    container    run    --restart=POLICY
[OPTIONS]  IMAGE[:TAG]

[COMMAND]  [ARG...]
```

For example, to start a container with a restart action of always, we use the command:

```
docker container run -restart=always -t -i -
name debian debian:latest /bin/bash
```

The restart flag accepts three main parameters:

- Always: Allows to the container to automatically restart the container no matter the exit return code.

- No: Prevents the container from restart in case of failure

- On-failure: Allows containers to restart on failure as long exit code is non-zero

You can set the number of failures in which the container should restart by passing the argument **-restart=on-failure:<number of failures>**

You may encounter an instance where the restart policies provided by Docker are not meeting your requirements. For such cases, you can use system process tools such as system, upstart, etc.

How To Mount Host Devices On A Container

Sometimes we might want to mount a host device on a container. For that, we use the –device flag following the run command. You can also bind-mount it using the **-v** option that also requires **–privileged** option.

The general syntax to mount a host device on a container is:

```
docker     container     run     --device=<Host
Device>:<Container Device

Mapping>:<Permissions>     [OPTIONS]     IMAGE
[COMMAND] [ARG...]
```

For example, if we want to mount a partition under /sda2 we can use the command;

```
docker          container          run          --
device=/dev/sda2:/dev/abc -i -t -name debian
debian:latest /bin/bash
```

Injecting Processes To Running Containers

Sometimes we may need to perform debugging tasks inside an already running container. Although there are external tools for such tasks, such as the nsenter tool that allows developers to enter into a namespace of a running process and execute commands, Docker has commands for such actions.

https://www.man7.org/linux/man-pages/man1/nsenter.1.html

Using the docker exec command, we can execute commands on running containers. The general syntax for the command is:

```
docker exec [OPTIONS] CONTAINER COMMAND [ARG]
```

For example, we can inject bash on an apache container using the commands:

```
docker container run -d nginx
docker container exec -i -t /bin/bash
```

The docker container exec command functions by entering the container namespace; once there, it starts a new process using the program specified.

Container Metadata

Using the Docker inspect command, we can fetch a container's metadata, which will help in the debugging processes.

The general syntax for the Docker inspect command is

```
docker inspect [OPTIONS] NAME|ID [NAME|ID...]
```

Let us create a new container and inspect its metadata:

```
$ id=$(sudo docker run -d -i debian /bin/bash)

Unable to find image 'debian:latest' locally

latest: Pulling from library/debian

376057ac6fa1: Pulling fs layer

376057ac6fa1: Verifying Checksum

376057ac6fa1: Download complete

376057ac6fa1: Pull complete
```

```
Digest:
sha256:4ab3309ba955211d1db92f405be609942b595a
720de789286376f030502ffd6f

Status:    Downloaded    newer    image    for
debian:latest
```

Once executed Docker, should give you detailed information about the container:

```
[
    {
        "Id":
"b8f955bdd622ddf13f1e1b015a59af6f557d2ce314c8
c88460ab66656e87def8",
        "Created":                    "2020-05-
27T01:03:17.806375367Z",|
        "Path": "/bin/bash",
        "Args": [],
        "State": {
            "Status": "running",
            "Running": true,
            "Paused": false,
            "Restarting": false,
            "OOMKilled": false,
            "Dead": false,
            "Pid": 14269,
```

```
        "ExitCode": 0,

        "Error": "",

        "StartedAt":                "2020-05-
27T01:03:20.018788249Z",

        "FinishedAt":               "0001-01-
01T00:00:00Z"

    },

    "Image":
"sha256:5971ee6076a06b695a62d8dbb5e4c977f2db1
e45902f5bb8d4b74511d9649dde",

---OUTPUT TRUNCATED---
```

After the execution of the command, Docker fetches the container metadata and outputs it in JSON format. You can use the -f flag to specify the format in which to print the metadata.

Section 5: Working with Docker Images

Docker images are the main building blocks of docker and docker containers. As we have covered in the containers section, docker images provide all the required layers used to create the containers.

Using docker images and the requirements of the application to deploy, you can use public images created by Docker or private parties, you can also create docker images as we will cover in this section.

In this section, we are going to cover docker images elements such as how to create docker images from a container, creating a docker hub account, removing images, exporting and importing images, and more.

Let us get started.

Although we may be using different operating systems, concepts discussed in this section will work on any system.

Docker Images From Containers

There are various ways to create a docker image for later use. One way is by making changes to an existing container and committing the image. You can also create docker images from Dockerfile, which we will discuss in later sections.

As we discussed in previous sections, when creating a new container, a read/write layer becomes attached to the container. However, this layer becomes automatically destroyed unless saved by the user.

Let us start by learning how to save the read/write layer and then create an image from an already created container.

To create a new image from the docker container's changes, we use the docker container command. The general syntax for the command is:

```
docker container commit [OPTIONS] CONTAINER
[REPOSITORY[:TAG]]
```

Let us start by creating a new container from scratch; you can create any image you prefer, such as debian, Ubuntu, centos, arch, etc.

```
sudo docker container run -it --name ubuntu
ubuntu
root@ae98215355cf:/#
```

Once you have the container created, in the terminal, update the repositories within the container using the container's default package manager.

```
root@ae98215355cf:/# apt-get update
```

Next, install a package of your choice such as LAMP stack (Linux Apache MySQL and PHP) as shown:

Step 1

Install the apache package and follow the configurations to set it up:

```
apt-get install apache2 apache2-doc
```

Step 2

Install MySQL packages on the system

```
apt-get install mysql-server mysql-client
libmysqlclient-dev

Step 3: Install PHP on your system using the
commands:

apt-get install libapache2-mod-php7.0 php7.0
php7.0-common php7.0-curl php7.0-dev php7.0-
gd php-pear php-imagick php7.0-mcrypt php7.0-
mysql php7.0-ps php7.0-xsl
```

Step 3

Finally, install a database management tool such as PhpMyAdmin

```
apt-get install phpMyAdmin
```

Once completed and appropriately configured, we can create a new image with the LAMP stack installed on the image.

Open a new terminal window and enter the commands as shown. The docker container can be inactive or running. To create an image, use the container id instead of the container name:

```
$ sudo docker commit --author "Salem" --
message "Ubuntu with LAMP stack installed"
ae98215355cf ubuntu-lamp


sha256:a54af6f61b13ef9a4ae6ce1053d5a0ab8a3afd
f9a581712aa9805e525d8ac006
```

Next, you can view the images within the host:

```
$ sudo docker image ls -a

REPOSITORY              TAG                     IMAGE
ID              CREATED                 SIZE

ubuntu-lamp                             latest
a54af6f61b13            About  a  minute  ago
862MB

debian                                  latest
5971ee6076a0                11   days   ago
114MB

ubuntu                                  latest
1d622ef86b13                4    weeks   ago
73.9MB

hello-world                             latest
bf756fb1ae65                4    months   ago
13.3kB
```

As you can see, Docker creates an image from the container and gives it the name ubuntu-lamp. You pass your name as the author of the image and the message, providing information about the image.

Docker container become created from image layers where each layer becomes inherited from the parent layer. Since the layers are in read-only mode, a read-write layer becomes created, which allows us to perform modifications on the system such as performing package installations.

Since this layer becomes automatically cleaned upon stopping or destroying the container, we used the docker commit command to preserve it and create a docker image stored with other docker images.

To view all the changes of the container's filesystem from its parent image, we use the docker diff command:

```
$ sudo docker diff ae98215355cf

C /usr

C /usr/share

A /usr/share/applications

A /usr/share/applications/phpmyadmin.desktop

C /usr/share/apport

C /usr/share/apport/package-hooks

A                    /usr/share/apport/package-
hooks/source_mysql-8.0.py
```

```
A /usr/share/apport/package-hooks/apache2.py

A /usr/share/zoneinfo

A /usr/share/zoneinfo/NZ

A /usr/share/zoneinfo/Europe

A /usr/share/zoneinfo/Europe/Budapest

A /usr/share/zoneinfo/Europe/Paris

A /usr/share/zoneinfo/Europe/Sofia

A /usr/share/zoneinfo/Europe/Belfast

A /usr/share/zoneinfo/Europe/Bratislava

A /usr/share/zoneinfo/Europe/Minsk

A /usr/share/zoneinfo/Europe/Riga

A /usr/share/zoneinfo/Europe/Vatican

A /usr/share/zoneinfo/Europe/Jersey

A /usr/share/zoneinfo/Europe/London
```

...OUTPUT TRUNCATED...

This command displays all the changes that have occurred within the filesystem. You can output to a text file for later inspections and debugging.

The docker diff command append prefixes to the files and directories modified

- A: The A prefix indicates the addition of a directory or file to the filesystem

- C: This prefix indicates the specified file or directory has received modifications

- D: D prefix represents a deleted file or directory.

Unless specified, a docker container becomes automatically paused when the docker commit command is running.

You can find more information about docker commit on the official documentation:

https://docs.docker.com/engine/reference/commandline/container_commit/

How To Work With Docker Hub

In this section, we are going to discuss the docker hub. We shall talk about how to set up an account and to connect with the docker client in the command-line.

Docker-hub is a cloud-based public docker image registry for hosting both public and public images, collaborating with others, as well as share your custom images. Docker hub supports full integration with services such as GitHub and Bitbucket, which allows for automatic image builds.

Before using the docker hub, you will require a docker account. Docker hub gives a free plan for hosting both public and public image repositories. However, you may need to upgrade to a paid plan if you need more repositories.

To create an account, open your browser and navigate to https://hub.docker.com and create an account if you do not have one. You can log in if already created.

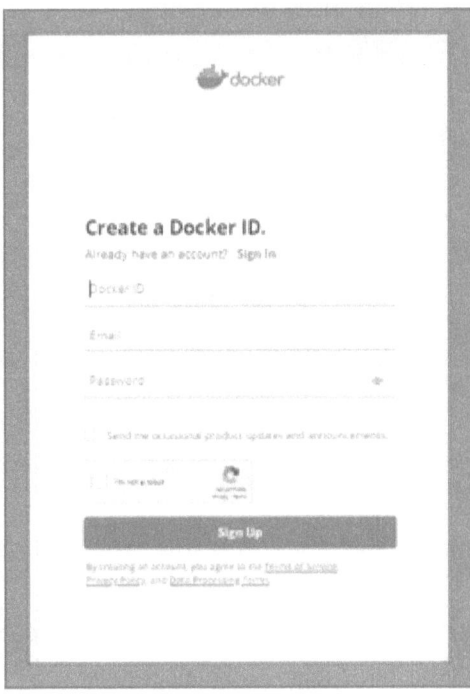

To have an account created, you will need to confirm your account using your email address. Finally, login, and you can start using the docker hub to publish images.

How To Work With Docker Registry

Throughout your docker journey, you will want to publish images to the Docker hub registry. Before pushing an image to docker hub, you will have to log in using your docker id or using a GitLab account. To log-in into docker hub, we use the docker login command.

The docker login command allows you to log-in into multiple docker registries at once and logout from specified servers using the docker logout command.

The general syntax for docker login and logout commands are:

```
docker login [OPTIONS] [SERVER]
```

```
docker logout [SERVER]
```

Calling the docker login and logout command automatically connects to a hub.docker.com server, but you can specify which server to use.

Let us learn how to log-in into docker default registry, gitlab hosted registry, view the stored login credentials, and log out from accounts.

To login into docker default registry, use this command:

Docker

```
$ sudo docker login
```

Login with your Docker ID to push and pull images from Docker Hub. If you don't have a Docker ID, head over to https://hub.docker.com to create one.

Username: <your docker id>

Password: <docker password>

WARNING! Your password will be stored unencrypted in /root/.docker/config.json.

Configure a credential helper to remove this warning. See

https://docs.docker.com/engine/reference/comm andline/login/#credentials-store

By default, docker login command uses interactive mode to get the credentials and log-in.

To view the stored log-in credentials, use docker info command and pipe the output to grep and search for Username and Registry:

```
sudo        docker        info        |        grep
^\(Username\|Registry\)
```

Username: artemis37

 Registry: https://index.docker.io/v1/

To log-in using a GitLab account, create an account on GitLab, and use the log-in credentials to log into Docker.

```
sudo docker login registry.gitlab.com

Username: artemis37

Password:

WARNING!  Your  password  will  be  stored
unencrypted in /root/.docker/config.json.

Configure a credential helper to remove this
warning. See

https://docs.docker.com/engine/reference/comm
andline/login/#credentials-store
```

To view all the store login credentials, dump the contents of the config.json file using the command:

```
sudo cat /root/.docker/config.json
{

        "auths": {

"https://index.docker.io/v1/": {

                        "auth":
"YXJ0ZW1pczM3OmhxRnJ1eEolPylBMnMlNg=="

                },

                "registry.gitlab.com": {

                        "auth":
"YXJ0ZW1pczM3OkM0Tj9FengzN1RfMzN3SA=="




                }

        },

        "HttpHeaders": {

                "User-Agent":        "Docker-
Client/19.03.9 (linux)"

        }

}
```

To logout on all the registries, use the docker logout command:

```
sudo docker logout
```

```
Removing       login       credentials       for
https://index.docker.io/v1/
```

To find out more information about docker logout command, use the –help flag.

How To Publish Docker Images To The Registry

Throughout the previous sections, we have downloaded images from the docker registry, which is a hub for sharing and publishing images.

In this section, we will see how to upload and publish our images to the official docker image-registry.

Before pushing an image to docker registry, ensure you are logged in to hub.docker.com using the local pc docker client. If you are using a third-party docker registry providers, check their login process on the official documentation.

To push a docker image to the registry, we use the docker push command. The general syntax for the command is:

Docker

```
docker image push [OPTIONS] [NAME]: [TAG]
docker push [OPTIONS] [NAME]:TAG
```

However, to push an image, we need to perform a few tasks such as tagging the image according to the publishing user. For example, docker image tag debian <publisher>/debian

Once we execute the command above, it will tag the debian image with the publisher/debian, and we can push the image to docker hub.

Next, we can publish our image to the docker hub registry using the docker image push command as shown:

```
sudo docker image push salem/debian
```

```
The      push      refers      to      repository
[docker.io/salem/debian]

8c02234b8605: Preparing

---code truncated.---
```

In some cases, Docker may deny access to the resource using the command-line, you can open the browser and create an image repository using the command provides:

The general syntax for the commands are:

89

```
docker       tag       local-image:tagname       new-
repo:tagname
```

```
docker push new-repo:tagname
```

The local-image refers to the name of the image you created or wish to push, followed by the tag name. Next, docker push command.

To find more information about working with Docker Hub images, check the documentation:

https://docs.docker.com/engine/reference/commandline/image_push/

How To Remove Docker Images

Similar to Docker containers, we can remove images hosted locally if not needed. To do this, we use the `docker image rm` command. The command removes the image or images passed to it. You can specify the image using the image's short or long id, the image's name and its tag, the image's digest value. If you specify the image's name and not tag, the latest tag becomes assumed by default and removes the latest image.

Docker

If the images within the local registry container have more than one tag, the tags will need removal before executing the docker image rm command. You can also remove them using -f or –force command which force-removes the images. This forces the removal of all the tags and images.

The general syntax for the command is:

```
docker image rm [OPTIONS] [IMAGES]
```

Let us start by viewing all the images within the registry

```
docker images ls.
```

```
REPOSITORY          TAG             IMAGE ID          CREATED
SIZE
salem/debian        latest          272093570a4e      35
minutes ago    114MB
debian              latest          272093570a4e      35
minutes ago    114MB
debian              <none>          5971ee6076a0      2 weeks
ago        114MB
ubuntu              latest          1d622ef86b13      5 weeks
ago        73.9MB
hello-world         latest          bf756fb1ae65      5 months
ago        13.3kB
```

Next, choose the image and remove it. You can use either of the image properties specified above. For this example, we are going to use the image id.

```
sudo docker image rm 272093570a4e
Error response from daemon: conflict: unable to delete 272093570a4e
(must be forced) - image is referenced in multiple repositories
```

Performing the above tasks fails as the image is referenced by other tags. You can remove all the image tags until the image is removed or use the force command.

```
sudo docker image rm --force 272093570a4e
Untagged: debian:latest
Untagged: salem/debian:latest
Deleted:
sha256:272093570a4ed5c6017382bc94f2db0e83a694582cf196a824f661641f49e6
4e
```

When using the –force command, ensure that the docker image you are trying to remove does not have any containers spawned to it, as this will lead to dangling images.

You can remove all images in the docker registry using the command:

```
docker image rm $(docker image rm -q)
```

To get more information on the docker rm command, use the -h flag, or check the official documentation:

https://docs.docker.com/engine/reference/commandline/image_rm/

How To Export Docker Images

Docker allows you to use tarballs and export the images for importation to other machines. This feature comes in handy if you do not want to use public images but export from a custom one. You can use the Docker save command to perform the task. The general syntax for the command is:

```
docker image save --output [filename.tar]
image [image name]
```

Let us start by pulling a new image. You can choose either. For this section, we will pull a new Redis image. Redis is an open-source data structure (in memory) used as a database cache or message broker.

Check more information about Redis from the source below:

https://redis.io/documentation

```
sudo docker pull redis
Using default tag: latest
latest: Pulling from library/redis
afb6ec6fdc1c: Pull complete
608641ee4c3f: Pull complete
668ab9e1f4bc: Pull complete
78a12698914e: Pull complete
d056855f4300: Pull complete
618fdf7d0dec: Pull complete
Digest:
sha256:d27740b5bd12087efc2b30ac9102fa767d6cc83611dc0fc28f0edb042e8359
96
Status: Downloaded newer image for redis:latest
docker.io/library/redis:latest
```

Once you have pulled an image of your choice, export the image as a tarball using the command:

```
docker image save --o=redis-image.tar redis
```

Executing the command creates a tar ball image within the current directory, with the image being importable to another host. We will discuss importing a docker image in later sections.

You can view the image using the ls -l command, as illustrated below:

```
sudo docker image save -o=redis-image.tar redis
sudo docker image ls
REPOSITORY          TAG            IMAGE ID          CREATED
SIZE
redis               latest         36304d3b4540      3 days
ago         104MB
hello-world         latest         bf756fb1ae65      5 months
ago         13.3kB
$ ls -l
total 105012
-rw------- 1 root root 107531264 Jun  1 15:05 redis-image.tar
```

The docker export command allows you to save a docker container filesystem using the commands:

```
docker export -o =container_name.tar name
```

```
sudo docker export -o=redis-container.tar loving_rubin
$ ls -l
total 206612
-rw------- 1 root root 104030720 Jun  1 15:10 redis-container.tar
-rw------- 1 root root 107531264 Jun  1 15:05 redis-image.tar
```

Check the docker export -h or docker container save -h command to view more information about usage.

How To Import Docker Tar Images

For Docker to use an image, it has to be stored locally. You can achieve this by pulling an image from the docker registry or by importing a docker tarball.

If you are exporting the image from a host that's different from the one that created it, you will need to download it using services such as FTP, SCP, or to specify a remote URL on the host.

However, since we are importing an image on the host that created it, we will simply use the docker import command. The general syntax is:

```
docker  image  import  [OPTIONS]  file|URL|-
[REPOSITORY[:TAG]]
```

Ensure the name to which the imported image does not conflict with an existing image name.

```
sudo  docker  import  redis-image.tar  redis-
imported:imported
```

```
sha256:e0ea41b7a9f7ca8e8d94acbfcab13a46d3f9ce44548e277b8c67545dc7823b
75
$ sudo docker image ls
REPOSITORY          TAG              IMAGE ID            CREATED
SIZE
redis-imported      imported         e0ea41b7a9f7        14
seconds ago      108MB
redis               latest           36304d3b4540        3 days
ago          104MB
hello-world         latest           bf756fb1ae65        5 months
ago          13.3kB
```

In the above the command, we imported the redis image using the name redis-imported and gave it a tag imported to avoid conflicts.

The docker import -h command is useful to learn more about importing images.

Working With Dockerfile

The dockerfile is an important Docker feature. Dockerfile is simply a text-based build-in tool that allows us to specify various properties about automating the process of creating Docker images.

The docker file is handled by the docker engine line through the line and performs tasks specified in the file one at a time. Docker images created a specified dockerfile are constant, which means they are immutable and cannot be changed.

Docker

Let us start by creating docker images with dockerfile. Before we begin the process, we need to perform various operations.

- Create an empty directory to the location of your choice within the filesystem and navigate to the created folder.

```
mkdir /home/debian/Docker_Folder
cd /home/debian/Docker_Folder/
```

- Next, start a file called dockerfile. You can use your favorite command to execute the operation.

```
touch Dockerfile && nano Dockerfile
```

- Once we have entered into nano or your specified text editor, enter the configuration as shown below:

```
# We use a Debian 10 image
FROM debian
# Create an author's name
LABEL maintainer= "Docker Author"
# Specify the container command
CMD /bin/bash
```

It's good to note that you can include more configuration to the Dockerfile; for instance, tag names, repositories, env, expose, volume, copy, user, onbuild, etc. For this tutorial, we stick to the basics.

- Next, execute the command in the directory that container the Dockerfile.

```
sudo docker image build .
```

```
Sending build context to Docker daemon  2.048kB
Step 1/3 : FROM debian
latest: Pulling from library/debian
376057ac6fa1: Pull complete
Digest:
sha256:4ab3309ba955211d1db92f405be609942b595a720de789286376f030502ffd
6f
Status: Downloaded newer image for debian:latest
 ---> 5971ee6076a0
Step 2/3 : LABEL maintainer="Docker Author"
 ---> Running in a36f19b77c7b
Removing intermediate container a36f19b77c7b
 ---> 625842ed3e5f
Step 3/3 : CMD /bin/bash
 ---> Running in 51ca2b43f2f5
Removing intermediate container 51ca2b43f2f5
 ---> fd164477471b
Successfully built fd164477471b
```

If you re-run the commands again, Docker reuses the intermediate layers from the images created in previous instances if there are no changes within the layers.

For more information about dockerfile config and build operations, check out the documentation on the topic.

https://docs.docker.com/reference/builder/#the-dockerignore-file.

https://docs.docker.com/engine/reference/builder/

Dockerfile Best Practices

Here, we are going to cover some of the best practices you should use when writing Docker files.

As we will see in the next section, Docker files are sensitive, especially when creating images and automated builds since docker builds are dependent on the contents of the Dockerfile.

A docker file, therefore, contains a specific format and set of pre-defined commands that allow developers to create specific images.

As mentioned earlier, a docker image contains read-only layers used to represent Dockerfile instructions. The layer in the image are stacked, with each represented as a delta of the changes from the adjacent layer.

For example, the docker file below adds new layers:

```
FROM debian:latest

COPY ./data

RUN make /data

CMD ruby /data/index.rb
```

Once you use an image and create a container from it, a new writeable layer, also called a container layer, is added on top of the existing layers. The writeable layers hold all the changes performed on the container, such as deleting files, changing permissions, creating new files, etc.

Some of the guidelines and recommended best practices include:

- Images created from a Docker file should generate short-lived containers. That means the containers should be stopped and destroyed, rebuilt and replaced within minimum configuration.

- A dockerfile should allow you to perform multi-stage builds.

You can find more information about Dockerfile best practices from the following reference link.

https://docs.docker.com/develop/develop-images/dockerfile_best-practices/

GitHub, Bitbucket – Automated Builds

We have covered how to use docker hub to create a static image build. However, docker hub allows us to use services such as GitHub and Bitbucket to create automated image builds. The repository should have a docker file along with the content that out to be added to the image. As usual, you will need docker hub id as well as GitHub account.

First, you need get to a docker file from your image of choice. You can use, Ubuntu, Debian, apache, nginx, redis, MongoDB etc. For this example, we will illustrate using a debian buster image and install nginx.

NOTE: The use of "various images" throughout the book is for diversity and meant to illustrate the power of Docker. If you prefer to use one image throughout the book, feel free to do so.

Open, your browser and navigate to the following resource page:

https://docs.nginx.com/nginx/admin-guide/installing-nginx/installing-nginx-docker/

Once you have the docker file created and the properties of the image specified, we can begin. You can also use the configuration given shown below:

```
FROM debain:latest

LABEL maintainer=" Docker Automater"

EXPOSE 80

RUN apt-get update && apt-get -y install nginx

CMD ["nginx", "-g", "daemon off;"]
```

Open http://hub.docker.com/ and login

Before creating automated builds, you need to link your github or bitbucket account with Docker. Go to "My Account Setting – Linked Accounts"

Once in the section, select the connect option. This will open the github login page and allow you to connect.

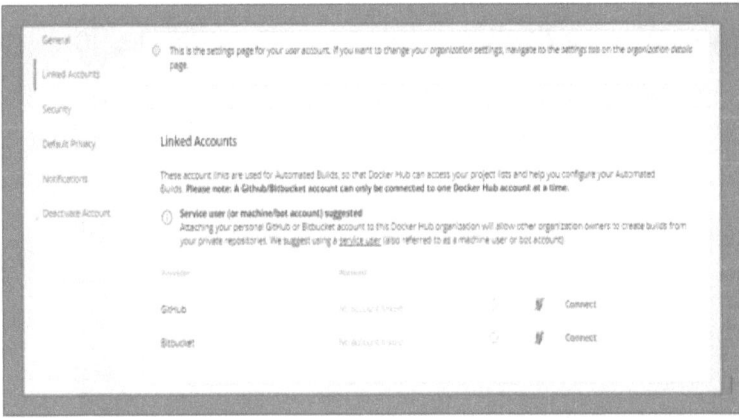

Once logged in to github, authorize the docker hub to your github account. If you have multiple organizations in your github account, select the request authorization to allow access to either and finally select authorize Docker.

Once comepleted, you will see your account connected to the Docker linked accounts section.

Next, we can create an automated build repository by selecting create repository.

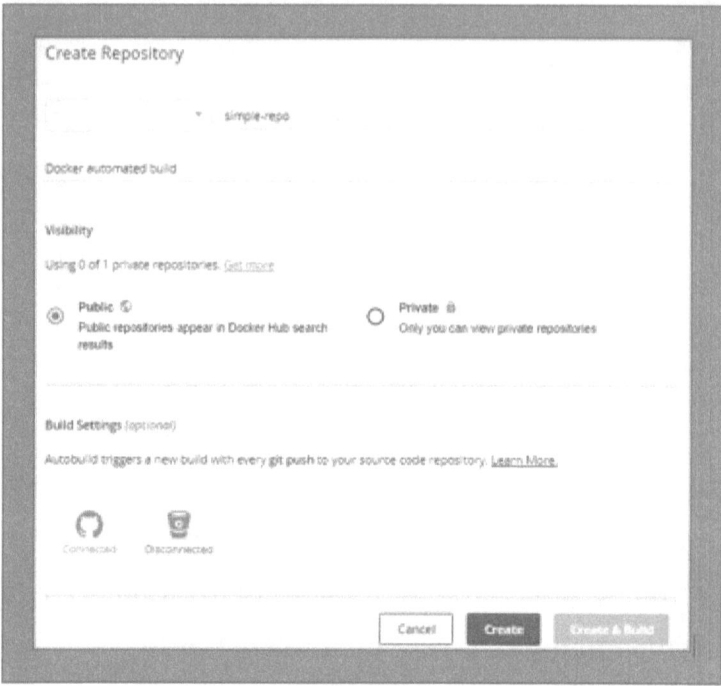

Once created, open the repository and navigate to build options. Select the connected account and configure your build configurations by selecting your github account and the source repository.

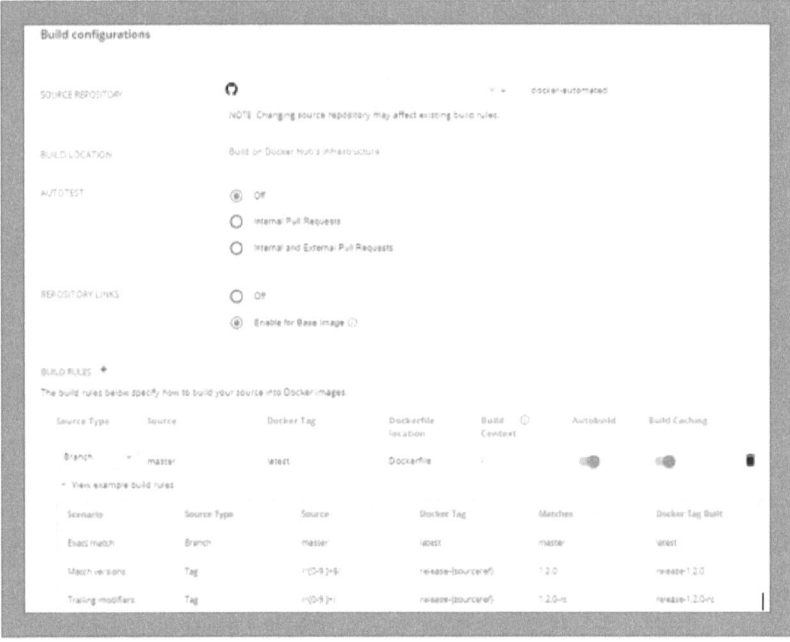

Once completed, select save and build. Ensure the github repository contains a Dockerfile uploaded. Once completed, this will start the build process using the Dockerfile configuration and triggers. You can also perform more automated build configurations by select configure automated builds option:

To check the status of the build, click on the docker tag and click on view logs for tasks such as debugging, the logs below show a failed docker build which can help you perform the necessary actions such as editing the docker file.

Section 6: Containers Network and Data Management

In this section, we are going to cover how to manage container networking and storage features. Among other things, shall look at

- How to work with containers outside the localhost,

- How to attach the docker containers to host systems,

- How to share data between the host and the containers, etc.

Throughout the book, we have only covered single containers and how to access them using the localhost. In the real world, cases change and the necessity to access containers outside the local network becomes more intense and increases the use of functionalities such as accessing external storages from the container, communicating with containers and more.

We will start by learning the basics of docker networking paradigms and setups, and finally cover more advanced networking concepts.

The Basics Of Containers Network And Data Management

By default, once a docker daemon starts, it creates a virtual Ethernet bridge called docker0. A network bridge refers to a network Link Layer between two network segments and allows for the sharing of traffic. Although a network bridge can be hardware or software-based, Docker uses the software version, which allows container connected to the same network bridge to communicate. Containers not connected to the same bridge are, however, isolated, with communication unsupported.

In Docker, you can configure user-based network bridges or use the default docker bridge. Let us get more information about the docker network bridge using the `ip addr` or `ifconfig` command as:

```
ip addr docker0
```

```
docker0: <NO-CARRIER,BROADCAST,MULTICAST,UP> mtu 1500 qdisc noqueue
state DOWN group default
    link/ether 02:42:88:48:49:fa brd ff:ff:ff:ff:ff:ff
    inet 172.17.0.1/16 brd 172.17.255.255 scope global docker0
       valid_lft forever preferred_lft forever
    inet6 fe80::42:88ff:fe48:49fa/64 scope link
       valid_lft forever preferred_lft forever
```

From the output above, we can see that the network bridge gets assigned the name docker0 as default configuration and has an IP address of 172.17.255.255. The docker bridge IP address and subnet is automatically configured by Docker using RFC 1918.

Learn more about the RFC 1918 here https://tools.ietf.org/html/rfc1918

Once a docker container becomes started, Docker automatically initializes a virtual run on ethernet bridge and performs actions such as:

- It connects one end of virtual ethernet pair to the default docker0 bridge interface in the main host

- It connects the other end of the virtual ethernet to the newly created container as its default ethernet eth0 network interface. Therefore, in the container, the virtual ethernet (veth0) is visible as eth0 and the main host is visible as veth0, veth1 or such.

Let us see this in example. Start a container using an image of your choice.

```
sudo   docker   container   run   -it--rm   -name
debian-container debian
```

Once the container becomes created and you are in the root shell, use the `ip addr` command. If you prefer to use the `ifconfig` command, you will need to install net-tools packages from the main repository.

```
ip addr | grep eth0
```

```
eth0@if11: <BROADCAST,MULTICAST,UP,LOWER_UP> mtu 1500 qdisc noqueue
state UP group default
    link/ether 02:42:ac:11:00:02 brd ff:ff:ff:ff:ff:ff link-netnsid 0
    inet 172.17.0.2/16 brd 172.17.255.255 scope global eth0
      valid_lft forever preferred_lft forever
```

The ethernet interface becomes assigned a value such as `eth0@if11` in which 11 or the value assigned to it corresponds to one end of the virtual ethernet pair. You can use this end value to identify the host end of the virtual ethernet pair in the docker host.

Similarly, the containers default ethernet interface (not loopback), becomes assigned the IP address such as 172.17.0.2 which is a subnet of the docker0, which is 172.17.0.1/16

Docker

If you close the container terminal and back to the main host, you will see a new network interface with a queer name. The name of the interface may change based on where the host is and hosted and the running OS. For example:

```
ip addr
```

```
ens4: flags=4163<UP, BROADCAST, RUNNING, MULTICAST>  mtu 1460
        inet 10.142.0.9  netmask 255.255.255.255  broadcast
10.142.0.9
        inet6 fe80::4001:aff:fe8e:9  prefixlen 64  scopeid 0x20<link>
        ether 42:01:0a:8e:00:09  txqueuelen 1000   (Ethernet)
        RX packets 22011  bytes 281869581 (268.8 MiB)
        RX errors 0  dropped 0  overruns 0  frame 0
        TX packets 17324  bytes 1770138 (1.6 MiB)
        TX errors 0  dropped 0 overruns 0  carrier 0  collisions 0
```

On the host, the interface ens4 or vnetxxxx@if4 is what's displayed. The value at the end of the interface name shows the other end of the virtual ethernet pair.

Value of 16 becomes assigned to the containers' network namespaces and is thus undisplayable on the main host. The name of the virtual ethernet pair becomes automatically generated by the Docker engine using a pair of seven-digit hex numbers.

For example, a8c40d9 while ensuring that the number is unique in the host. The virtual ethernet is bound to dockero default ethernet bridge.

We can create more containers and inspect the dockero bridge. You can connect to the host network stack by passing --network=host flag.

Once you have this specified, the host ends of the virtual ethernet pair become automatically connected to the dockero bridge. Docker sets up the dockero bridge as well as creating iptables for NAT interface, allowing all the containers to connect externally by default. However, this action is one way, and no external access to the container is allowed.

Check the Docker's host iptables.

```
sudo iptables -t nat -n -L
```

```
Chain PREROUTING (policy ACCEPT)
target     prot opt source              destination
DOCKER     all  --  0.0.0.0/0           0.0.0.0/0
ADDRTYPE match dst-type LOCAL

Chain INPUT (policy ACCEPT)
target     prot opt source              destination

Chain POSTROUTING (policy ACCEPT)
target     prot opt source              destination
MASQUERADE all  --  172.17.0.0/16       0.0.0.0/0

Chain OUTPUT (policy ACCEPT)
target     prot opt source              destination
DOCKER     all  --  0.0.0.0/0           !127.0.0.0/8
ADDRTYPE match dst-type LOCAL

Chain DOCKER (2 references)
target     prot opt source          |   destination
RETURN     all  --  0.0.0.0/0           0.0.0.0/0
```

As shown, the POSTROUTING iptables rule is under the configuration of the 172.17.0.0/16 subnet. This rule changes the source IP address of the data packets from 172.17.0.0/16 subnet to the IP address of the host. This subnet becomes assigned to dockero network bridge. This rule also allows containers to communicate externally.

Test the external communication with traceroute or ping as shown below:

```
ping google.com
```

```
64 bytes from vw-in-f101.1e100.net (173.194.217.101): icmp_seq=4
ttl=52 time=0.995 ms
64 bytes from vw-in-f101.1e100.net (173.194.217.101): icmp_seq=5
ttl=52 time=1.03 ms
64 bytes from vw-in-f101.1e100.net (173.194.217.101): icmp_seq=6
ttl=52 time=0.980 ms
64 bytes from vw-in-f101.1e100.net (173.194.217.101): icmp_seq=7
ttl=52 time=1.51 ms
64 bytes from vw-in-f101.1e100.net (173.194.217.101): icmp_seq=8
ttl=52 time=1.12 ms
64 bytes from vw-in-f101.1e100.net (173.194.217.101): icmp_seq=9
ttl=52 time=1.25 ms
```

That illustrates the container is accessible from the outside world. Unfortunately, the container is still inaccessible to the outside world. Hosted services such as apache, nginx etc. still need to be accessed from the outside world. In the next section, we will cover how to access a container externally.

How To Work With Container External Access

As we have seen, Docker allows containers to send traffic to the external world. However, the reverse is not true. Although this is not a default configuration, Docker still provides solutions for services within a container to be accessed externally.

A collection of services work together to provide a microservice architecture. Docker plays a crucial role by enabling microservice architecture due to it being lightweight.

https://microservices.io/

Docker allows us to pass the main options to the docker container run command to perform various tasks.

- –p or --publish - publishes all the ports of the container to the host.

- -P or --publish-all - publishes all the exposed ports of the container to random ports.

Docker

Either of the commands above allows the container to become accessible from the outside world and the services running.

Let's illustrate the above concept with an example. We will create an nginx service using an nginx image and map the service to be accessed from the port 80.

```
sudo docker run -d -p 80:80 nginx
```

We can view the container port mapping to the main docker host using the docker port commands.

```
docker container port <container id>
```

For example, to view the ports mapped to the host ports, we can use the commands as shown below:

```
sudo docker container port 24f3ffd378f7

80/tcp -> 0.0.0.0:80
```

This command confirms that the port 80 of the docker container has mapped to port 80 of the host. The 0.0.0.0 refers to any 1P address within the subnet of the dockers host.

Having this allows you to connect to the nginx service we created using the dockers host IP address and the port number mapped to it. For example, performing a basic http curl request should do the trick as:

```
curl -a 172.17.0.1:80
```

```
<!DOCTYPE html>
<html>
<head>
<title>Welcome to nginx!</title>
<style>
    body {
        width: 35em;
        margin: 0 auto;
        font-family: Tahoma, Verdana, Arial, sans-serif;
    }
</style>
</head>
<body>
<h1>Welcome to nginx!</h1>
<p>If you see this page, the nginx web server is successfully installed and
working. Further configuration is required.</p>

<p>For online documentation and support please refer to
<a href="http://nginx.org/">nginx.org</a>.<br/>
Commercial support is available at
<a href="http://nginx.com/">nginx.com</a>.</p>

<p><em>Thank you for using nginx.</em></p>
</body>
</html>
```

Once the container launches using the -p followed by the <host port>:<container port>, the docker engine configures iptables destination rules. This NAT rule is in charge of configuring the packet forwarding received on Docker's host port to the container port. For example, you can map the host port to 8080 or other random port as long as it's not occupied.

View the iptables rules using the command:

```
sudo iptables -t nat -n -L
```

```
---OUTPUT TRUNCATED---
Chain DOCKER (2 references)
target     prot opt source           destination
RETURN     all  --  0.0.0.0/0        0.0.0.0/0
DNAT       tcp  --  0.0.0.0/0        0.0.0.0/0          tcp
dpt:80 to:172.17.0.2:80
```

The NAT rule created by the docker engine has various configurations such as:

- Source IP address: This specifies the source IP address, thus allowing that source IP to receive packets. By default, this is a wildcard address 0.0.0.0/0

- Destination IP address: This specifies that the rule is valid to all packets received on any interface on the dockers host. Wildcard address 0.0.0.0/0 is used.

- Destination Port: Allows the iptables to apply this rule to only the packets received on port 80. For our example, dpt:80 is what becomes used.

- Forwarding IP address: Points to the container's ip address and the port to which the packets will become forwarded to, provided it meets the set requirements.

The docker -p command allows us o pass more arguments while allowing external access to the container service. For example:

- `<ContainerPort>`: This configuration allows you to set only the container port and allow Docker to select a port on the dockers host automatically. This port has to be within the range of 32768 and 60999. The port range are defined in `/proc/sys/net/ipv4/ip_local_port_range`

- `<ip>` `<hostPort>` `<ContainerPort>`: This configuration allows us to explicitly specify an IP interface on dockers host.

- `<IP >::<ContainerPort>` :Allows us to specify the IP address on dockers host while allowing Docker to select a port on the dockers host automatically.

If you, however, use the -P flag, the docker container run command maps out all the port from the image's metadata used to create the container to random high-order port

(32768 to 60999) in the dockers host. The image port metadata becomes created using the EXPOSE option of a Dockerfile.

You can find more information on docker networking from the resource page below:

https://docs.docker.com/engine/userguide/networking/

Container IP Sharing

By default, once a container becomes launched, the docker engine automatically gives it an IP address. You can use host network mode to attach the container to the host IP address or none network mode to initialize the container with no network.

However, for certain services, you may need to share a single IP address. Although you can run multiple services on a single container, as a recommendation, you should host services on various containers and share the IP address instead.

You can think of it as a container IP and the IP shared across the specified services within various containers.

Docker

Let us start by launching a container in the background as shown below

```
sudo    docker    container    run    -itd    --
name=mainContainer debian
```

In the above command, we create a debian container and call it the main container. Let us inspect the IP address of the container.

sudo docker exec mainContainer ip addr

```
1: lo: <LOOPBACK,UP,LOWER_UP> mtu 65536 qdisc noqueue state UNKNOWN
group default qlen 1000
    link/loopback 00:00:00:00:00:00 brd 00:00:00:00:00:00
    inet 127.0.0.1/8 scope host lo
       valid_lft forever preferred_lft forever
8: eth0@if9: <BROADCAST,MULTICAST,UP,LOWER_UP> mtu 1500 qdisc noqueue
state UP group default
    link/ether 02:42:ac:11:00:03 brd ff:ff:ff:ff:ff:ff link-netnsid 0
    inet 172.17.0.3/16 brd 172.17.255.255 scope global eth0
       valid_lft forever preferred_lft forever
```

Next, we launch a new container and attach its network to the mainContainer Ip address, and view the IP address attached to the container.

```
sudo    docker    container    run    --rm    --net
container:mainContainer debian ip addr
```

```
1: lo: <LOOPBACK,UP,LOWER_UP> mtu 65536 qdisc noqueue state UNKNOWN
group default qlen 1000
    link/loopback 00:00:00:00:00:00 brd 00:00:00:00:00:00
    inet 127.0.0.1/8 scope host lo
       valid_lft forever preferred_lft forever
8: eth0@if9: <BROADCAST,MULTICAST,UP,LOWER_UP> mtu 1500 qdisc noqueue
state UP group default
    link/ether 02:42:ac:11:00:03 brd ff:ff:ff:ff:ff:ff link-netnsid 0
    inet 172.17.0.3/16 brd 172.17.255.255 scope global eth0
       valid_lft forever preferred_lft forever
```

As shown in the above outputs, we can see the eth0 of the main container and the transient container contains the same network interface indexes and shares the same IP address of 172.17.0.3

That works when one container becomes created, and the successive containers use the network of the main or first container, the docker-engine created a network namespace for the main container and then allocated the same network namespace to the other containers.

Its good to note that the main container network namespace should be running before creating other containers and sharing the network namespace. If the container stops before the 'slave' containers, it will put the containers in an unusable state.

This is a common concept used by containers inside a Kubernetes pod to share the IP address.

How To Work With User-Defined Network Bridges

Throughout the previous sections, we have used the default network bridge created by Docker upon installation. That allows the containers that we create to communicate with each using their IP address but the container names.

In a microservice architecture, linking containers with the ip addresses created during startup is not convenient. Docker came up with ways to link containers using user-defined network bridges.

User-defined network bridges are similar to the default docker network-bridge, with the primary difference being that they provide extra features such as:

- DNS based load balancing which is a feature that supports multicontainer communication and orchestration.

- Service discovery using embedded DNS server

- Subnet configuration on the specified bridge

- Manual allocation of container IP address from the defined bridge subnet.

Docker

In this section, we shall cover how to work with user-defined network bridges and learn more about how to use them.

We use the docker network command to perform network-based operations. The docker network command accepts these commands:

- `connect` - Connect a container to a network

- `create` - Create a network

- `disconnect` - Detach a specified container from a network

- `inspect` - Shows comprehensive information on one or more networks

- `ls` – Lists the available networks

- `prune` – used to remove all unused networks

- `rm` – used to remove one or more networks.

Let us create a network bridge and call it `bridge0` as shown in the commands below:

```
sudo docker network create bridge0
6f83ff1af4785192f2a57bd58e4396e60e9002eb51738
7bc09858a227459f9c4
```

Docker

We can inspect the `bridge0` interface configuration using the docker network inspect command as shown below:

```
sudo docker network inspect bridge0
```

```
[
    {
        "Name": "bridge0",
        "Id":
"6f83ff1af4785192f2a57bd58e4396e60e9002eb517387bc09858a227459f9c4",
        "Created": "2020-06-02T03:47:43.525930291Z",
        "Scope": "local",
        "Driver": "bridge",
        "EnableIPv6": false,
        "IPAM": {
            "Driver": "default",
            "Options": {},
            "Config": [
                {
                    "Subnet": "172.18.0.0/16",
                    "Gateway": "172.18.0.1"
                }
            ]
        },
        "Internal": false,
        "Attachable": false,
        "Ingress": false,
        "ConfigFrom": {
            "Network": ""
        },
        "ConfigOnly": false,
        "Containers": {},
        "Options": {},
        "Labels": {}
    }
]
```

From the configuration, we see that the network bridge gets assigned a subnet of 172.18.0.0./16 and a default gateway of 172.18.0.1.

You can also view the bridge from the host using the ip addr command as:

```
ip addr
```

```
---OUTPUT TRUNCATED---
10: br-6f83ff1af478: <NO-CARRIER,BROADCAST,MULTICAST,UP> mtu 1500
qdisc noqueue state DOWN group default
    link/ether 02:42:66:46:b3:fc brd ff:ff:ff:ff:ff:ff
    inet 172.18.0.1/16 brd 172.18.255.255 scope global br-
6f83ff1af478
```

As we can see, a new network bridge with the name br-6f83ff1af478 becomes created and allocated an address of 172.18.0.1/16. The network bridge name becomes created by adding a br- prefix before the network id.

To understand more about the network bridge, you can view the iptables configurations using the following command:

sudo iptables -t nat -n –L

```
---OUTPUT TRUNCATED---
Chain POSTROUTING (policy ACCEPT)
target       prot opt source             destination
MASQUERADE   all  --  172.18.0.0/16      0.0.0.0/0
MASQUERADE   all  --  172.17.0.0/16      0.0.0.0/0
```

As you can see, a POSTROUTING rule becomes added for 172.18.0.0/16 subnet similar to the docker default bridge.

Container Service Discovery And Load Balancing

We have seen how to work with user-defined bridges and their benefits. To better illustrate their capabilities as well as cover load balancing and network discovery, we will create a container-like topology.

We will create two containers as services and use a transient container to illustrate service discovery via embedded DNS and DNS based load balancing capabilities of user-defined network bridges.

Begin by creating two containers and connecting them to the network bridge we created earlier using the docker run command as shown below:

```
sudo docker container run -it -d --name
slaveContainer1 --network-alias slaveAlias --
net bridge0 debian

sudo docker container run -it -d --name
slaveContainer2 --network-alias slaveAlias --
net bridge0 debian
```

We use the –network alias to group multiple containers under a single name allowing load balancing them with embedded DNS, which uses round-robin load balancing.

https://www.cloudflare.com/learning/dns/glossary/round-robin-dns/

https://www.nginx.com/resources/glossary/round-robin-load-balancing/

Next, we can inspect the two containers' IP addresses using the inspect command:

```
sudo docker inspect -format
'{{.NetworkSettings.Networks.bridge0.IPAddress
}}' slaveContainer1

172.18.0.2

sudo docker inspect --format '{{
.NetworkSettings.Networks.bridge0.IPAddress
}}' slaveContainer2

172.18.0.3
```

We used the NetworkSettings.Network.bridgeo.IPAddress to filter only the IP address of the containers and not the entire configuration.

Next, we can use a transient container to test for service discovery on user-defined bridges.

```
sudo docker run --net bridge0 --rm debian
ping slaveContainer1
```

```
PING slaveContainer1 (172.18.0.2) 56(84) bytes of data.
64 bytes from slaveContainer1.bridge0 (172.18.0.2): icmp_seq=1 ttl=64
time=0.154 ms
64 bytes from slaveContainer1.bridge0 (172.18.0.2): icmp_seq=2 ttl=64
time=0.089 ms
64 bytes from slaveContainer1.bridge0 (172.18.0.2): icmp_seq=3 ttl=64
time=0.075 ms
64 bytes from slaveContainer1.bridge0 (172.18.0.2): icmp_seq=4 ttl=64
time=0.075 ms

--- slaveContainer1 ping statistics ---
4 packets transmitted, 4 received, 0% packet loss, time 43ms
rtt min/avg/max/mdev = 0.075/0.098/0.154/0.033 ms
```

```
sudo docker run --net bridge0 --rm debian
ping slaveContainer2
```

```
PING slaveContainer2 (172.18.0.3) 56(84) bytes of data.
64 bytes from slaveContainer2.bridge0 (172.18.0.3): icmp_seq=1 ttl=64
time=0.100 ms
64 bytes from slaveContainer2.bridge0 (172.18.0.3): icmp_seq=2 ttl=64
time=0.077 ms
64 bytes from slaveContainer2.bridge0 (172.18.0.3): icmp_seq=3 ttl=64
time=0.099 ms
64 bytes from slaveContainer2.bridge0 (172.18.0.3): icmp_seq=4 ttl=64
time=0.080 ms

--- slaveContainer2 ping statistics ---
4 packets transmitted, 4 received, 0% packet loss, time 62ms
rtt min/avg/max/mdev = 0.077/0.089/0.100/0.010 ms
```

Finally, the containers can now communicate with each other using their names, which helps improve the concept of multi containers.

Let us take DNS load balancing for a spin. We can use the network net alias ping to illustrate this —shown in the command below.

```
sudo docker container run --net bridge0 --rm
debian ping -c4 slaveAlias
```

```
PING slaveAlias (172.18.0.3) 56(84) bytes of data.
64 bytes from slaveContainer2.bridge0 (172.18.0.3): icmp_seq=1 ttl=64
time=0.145 ms
64 bytes from slaveContainer2.bridge0 (172.18.0.3): icmp_seq=2 ttl=64
time=0.078 ms
64 bytes from slaveContainer2.bridge0 (172.18.0.3): icmp_seq=3 ttl=64
time=0.083 ms
64 bytes from slaveContainer2.bridge0 (172.18.0.3): icmp_seq=4 ttl=64
time=0.079 ms

--- slaveAlias ping statistics ---
4 packets transmitted, 4 received, 0% packet loss, time 52ms
rtt min/avg/max/mdev = 0.078/0.096/0.145/0.029 ms
```

```
sudo docker container run --net bridge0 --rm
debian ping -c4 slaveAlias
```

```
PING slaveAlias (172.18.0.2) 56(84) bytes of data.
64 bytes from slaveContainer1.bridge0 (172.18.0.2): icmp_seq=1 ttl=64
time=0.094 ms
64 bytes from slaveContainer1.bridge0 (172.18.0.2): icmp_seq=2 ttl=64
time=0.078 ms
64 bytes from slaveContainer1.bridge0 (172.18.0.2): icmp_seq=3 ttl=64
time=0.079 ms
64 bytes from slaveContainer1.bridge0 (172.18.0.2): icmp_seq=4 ttl=64
time=0.078 ms

--- slaveAlias ping statistics ---
4 packets transmitted, 4 received, 0% packet loss, time 83ms
rtt min/avg/max/mdev = 0.078/0.082/0.094/0.009 ms
```

BOOM! It works!

As we can see from the above outputs, the first ping got a response from 172.18.0.3, and the second ping got a reponse from 172.18.0.3, which shows that the DNS load balancer is working and resolves the slaveAlias alias using a round-robin algorithm.

Once a container becomes created and connected to the user-defined network bridge, Docker automatically adds the name of the container and its alias to the DNS record of the user-defined network. It then propagates the details to other containers connected to the same user-defined network bridge via the embeded DNS on 127.0.0.11

Since its DNS server like any other, we can query the DNS records using tools such as dig or nslookup. Debian base image does not come with the tool installed and may require you to install it.

```
sudo docker container run -rm -it --net
bridge0 debian

root@32ec297c52cc:/# apt-get update

apt-get install dnsutils -y
```

```
root@32ec297c52cc:/# dig slaveAlias

; <<>> DiG 9.11.5-P4-5.1+deb10u1-Debian <<>> slaveAlias
;; global options: +cmd
;; Got answer:
;; ->>HEADER<<- opcode: QUERY, status: NOERROR, id: 50275
;; flags: qr rd ra; QUERY: 1, ANSWER: 2, AUTHORITY: 0, ADDITIONAL: 0

;; QUESTION SECTION:
;slaveAlias.                    IN      A

;; ANSWER SECTION:
slaveAlias.             600    IN      A       172.18.0.3
slaveAlias.             600    IN      A       172.18.0.2

;; Query time: 0 msec
;; SERVER: 127.0.0.11#53(127.0.0.11)
;; WHEN: Tue Jun 02 05:19:26 UTC 2020
;; MSG SIZE  rcvd: 80
```

As seen, the DNS record has two IP addresses 172.18.0.3, 2 as
A records. Although DNS based load balancing is important,
services such as nginx may not benefit much from them due
to various factors.

Working With Container Volumes

At this point, you should be familiar with the Docker
read/write layer and that it's temporary and cleared upon
container removal.

However, in some cases, you may need to preserve data
beyond the life-cycle of the container. Although we can use
Docker commit to ensure we keep the data, this may cause
the image to become bloated, which may hinder deployment

processes. That is where data persistence comes into play. We use volumes mounted outside the container filesystem or bind mounts.

Docker volume is a directory or directories within the docker host. Docker creates and manages them and can be mounted on to our container and have all the applications store information in the volume. The docker volumes are named or anonymous and automatically generated. There are features such as docker volume plugins that add more functionality. The scope of docker plugins is beyond the scope of the book.

Let us start by creating a docker volume using the docker volume create command as shown below:

```
sudo docker volume create dataVolume

dataVolume
```

You can view the available containers using the docker volume ls command: One is an anonymous container while the other is named.

```
sudo docker volume ls
```

```
DRIVER              VOLUME NAME
local
1fcd1967e3d30876233958c67e330c8d6e1a12050e475bdb01cb400eb127c698
local               dataVolume
```

Docker

Next, we can create a docker container in an interactive mode to mount the volume.

```
sudo    docker    container    run    -it    -v
dataVolume:/usr/data
```

Once mounted, we can navigate to the directory.

Next, we can create a sample file and place some information into it.

```
root@c61187dec76c:/usr/data# echo "Hello, world!" > hello.txt
root@c61187dec76c:/usr/data# cat hello.txt
Hello, world!
```

Finally, exit from the contaier and remove it using the docker rm command. Next, create a new container and mount the dataVolume volume as we did in the previous section

```
sudo    docker    container    run    -it    --name
debianMounted   -v dataVolume:/usr/data debian
```

```
root@b0f658c6e203:/# cd /usr
root@b0f658c6e203:/usr# ls -l
total 36
drwxr-xr-x  2 root root 4096 May 14 14:50 bin
drwxr-xr-x  2 root root 4096 Jun  2 06:16 data
drwxr-xr-x  2 root root 4096 May  2 16:39 games
drwxr-xr-x  3 root root 4096 May 14 14:50 include
drwxr-xr-x 10 root root 4096 May 14 14:50 lib
drwxr-xr-x 10 root root 4096 May 14 14:50 local
drwxr-xr-x  2 root root 4096 May 14 14:50 sbin
drwxr-xr-x 32 root root 4096 May 14 14:50 share
drwxr-xr-x  2 root root 4096 May  2 16:39 src
root@b0f658c6e203:/usr# cd data
root@b0f658c6e203:/usr/data# ls -l
total 4
-rw-r--r-- 1 root root 14 Jun  2 06:17 hello.txt
root@b0f658c6e203:/usr/data# cat hello.txt
Hello, world!
root@b0f658c6e203:/usr/data#
```

As we can see, the data becomes saved in the volume and
mounted to new containers as specified by the user. You can
view the volume save path using the Docker inspect
command as:

```
sudo docker volume inspect dataVolume
```

```
[
    {
        "CreatedAt": "2020-06-02T06:16:40Z",
        "Driver": "local",
        "Labels": {},
        "Mountpoint": "/var/lib/docker/volumes/dataVolume/_data",
        "Name": "dataVolume",
        "Options": {},
        "Scope": "local"
    }
]
```

Docker

As we can see, the volume mounting is under
`/var/lib/docker/volumes/dataVolume/_data.` We
can view the graphical representation using tree, etc.

Let us create new demo data.

```
sudo   docker   container   run   -it   --name
debianMounted  -v dataVolume:/usr/data debian


root@ea0e4743c228:/# cd /usr/data/

root@ea0e4743c228:/usr/data# ls -l

total 4

-rw-r--r-- 1 root  root  14  Jun   2  06:17
hello.txt

root@ea0e4743c228:/usr/data# mkdir dir1 dir2
dir3   dir4   &&   touch   dir1/file1.txt
dir2/file2.txt dir3/file3.txt dir4/file4.txt

root@ea0e4743c228:/usr/data# ls -l

total 20

drwxr-xr-x 2 root root 4096 Jun  2 06:29 dir1
```

```
drwxr-xr-x 2 root root 4096 Jun  2 06:29 dir2

drwxr-xr-x 2 root root 4096 Jun  2 06:29 dir3

drwxr-xr-x 2 root root 4096 Jun  2 06:29 dir4

-rw-r--r-- 1 root  root     14 Jun   2 06:17
hello.txt

root@ea0e4743c228:/usr/data# tree

.

|-- dir1
|    `-- file1.txt
|-- dir2
|    `-- file2.txt
|-- dir3
|    `-- file3.txt
|-- dir4
|    `-- file4.txt
`-- hello.txt


4 directories, 5 files
```

The same concept applies when sharing data between a host and a container. You need to mount a directory instead of a docker volume. Find more information about docker volumes from the resource page below:

https://docs.docker.com/storage/volumes/

Data Sharing Between Host And Container

In previous sections, we covered how to create volumes and mount them to containers, thus allowing us to store data continually after the removal of a container and also share data between containers.

In this sub-section, we are going to go over how to use bind mount to mount a directory within the main host and share data with containers using the directory as a mount point.

Before we start, ensure you have docker daemon running and that you have the permissions to execute commands.

Next, we will start by creating a directory in the main hosts home directory called bind_data as shown:

```
mkdir ~/bind_data
```

Navigate to the bind_data directory and create a new file with some information.

```
cd ~/bind_data

touch bind_demo.txt && echo "Hello, world bind demo" > bind_demo.txt
```

Next, we create a container and mount the directory we created above and view the contents of the bind_demo.txt file.

You can use any image you prefer to mount the directory. Here, we shall be using Debian.

```
docker container run -rm -v ~/bind_data:/data
debian cat /data/bind_demo.txt

Hello, world bind demo
```

That shows how to share data from a docker container to the Docker host. Although this is a simple technique, it's very powerful and comes in handy in large scale environments.

Launching a container with the -v flag followed by the host path: container path option allows the docker engine bind to mount the host path into the container filesystem using the path provided. The bind mount is a Linux functionality that allows for the mapping of existing directory structures into different locations.

You can find more information on Linux mount options from the page link below:

https://www.man7.org/linux/man-
pages/man8/mount.8.html

Using Docker Tmpfs Mounts

The two main ways to share data between the host and containers are using volumes or bind mounts that keep data after the removal of a container. However, running Docker on Linux provides a third option: *using the tmpfs mounts.*

Launching a container with tmpfs creates files outside the containers read/write layer. However, unlike volumes and bind mounts, tmpfs is a temporary virtual filesystem permitted only on the main host's memory.

This means that if a container launches with tmpfs, the mount point gets deleted with no data retained.

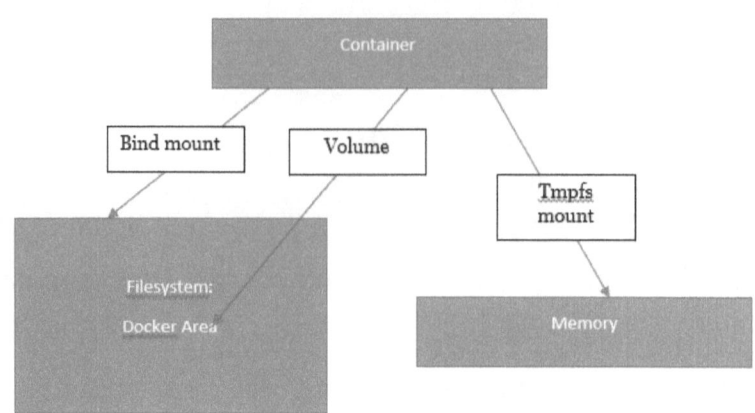

This feature is very useful while working with sensitive data that you do not want preserved in either host or container's read/write layer.

There are various limitations associated with running a container with tmpfs mounts. These include:

- Data is not shareable between containers while using tmpfs

- The tmpfs mount functionality is only available if Docker is running on a Linux system.

To mount a container with tmpfs, ensure you are running Linux and that the docker daemon is running, use the commands:

```
docker   run   -rm   -d   -it   -tmpfs   /data
debian:latest
```

You can verify that the mount point in the container is of type tmpfs by running a docker inspect command on the container as:

```
Docker container inspect <container name>
```

```
"Tmpfs": {

    "/data": ""

},
```

You can read more on tmpfs on:

https://www.man7.org/linux/man-pages/man5/tmpfs.5.html

Conclusion

We have completed our tutorial on Docker for beginners.

Docker is an advanced tool and very essential to every DevOps engineer. Although there are more advanced concepts not covered in this book, the content here should be more than enough to help you master working with Docker.

Thank you for reading this guide. I hope you found it immensely valuable.

I'd like your feedback. If you are happy with this book, please leave a review on Amazon.

Please leave a review for this book on Amazon by visiting the page below:

https://amzn.to/2VMR5qr

www.ingramcontent.com/pod-product-compliance
Lightning Source LLC
Chambersburg PA
CBHW030651220526
45463CB00005B/1727